# An Introduction to Professional Consulting

## The Art of Finding Clients and Securing Engagements

**Dan Grijzenhout**
**4/4/2016**

## DEDICATION

This book is dedicated to my son, David and daughter, Paige. Thank you both for always sticking by me.

I love you both.

-     Dan

# CONTENTS

# INTRODUCTION – WE ARE CONSULTANTS

There are many of us.

Some of us belong to professional consulting organizations, some of us are independents, some of us run our own consulting businesses, some do it full time, some part-time, some of us provide advice, some analyze and write reports, some help find resources, some do financial and investment work, others write code, build web-sites, and others physically design and build things.

But the bottom line is that we are brought in under contract to complete something for someone else, either as an individual or a business entity of some sort.

We are brought into a situation because we have the expertise, ability or the time to do something for another individual or company that they don't have themselves or internally within their organization. Or, they have seen or heard about us and our reputation is such that they just want us involved in what they are trying to construct.

This first book of mine on this topic is primarily pointed at the new practitioner involved in the world of business and IT consulting in general although there are aspects to what I am writing about that others might find to be useful knowledge as well. If you can think of anything you can do for any business entity under contract and get paid to do it, then that will fall within the scope of what I am writing about in this book.

In my next chapter, "An Introduction to Professional Consulting", I discuss the five core parts that my series of books on this topic will cover. This first book is intended to cover Parts One and Two:

Part One:  What It Means to Be a Consultant
Part Two:  Finding and Securing the Engagement

Within this book, I take the person through the decision process of whether or not to even consider becoming a consultant in the first place through to discussing niches you can become proficient in and make a living at within the professional consulting profession.  Then, I will show you ways that you can find clients for your services, that clients can find you, and ultimately how to secure an engagement for yourself or your team so you can start work.

Oh yes, I will also show you things you can do to help protect yourself financially while undertaking these projects should anything go wrong or sideways on the project.
Enjoy the book and best of luck with your consulting career.

- Dan Grijzenhout - Author

# AN INTRODUCTION TO PROFESSIONAL CONSULTING

**Professional Consulting** is an art form.

My complete professional consulting training series is built into five parts:

Part One:  What It Means to Be a Consultant
Part Two:  Finding and Securing the Engagement
Part Three:  Planning, Information Gathering, Current Analysis, Requirements and Gap Identification
Part Four:  Strategy Development, Architecture Definition and Project Identification
Part Five:  Migration Planning, Project Development and Dependencies, Resourcing, Durations and Timing

The core values and systems that define a corporation provide the high level boundaries that we as consultants work within to attempt to effect positive change, growth and profitability for those that employ us.  Our goal is to provide these corporations with exceptional results, to help them work smarter and to inspire their staff to achieve greatness.

When we achieve these goals and the staff are inspired, they will perform at their best and good things happen. They will take on big challenges, they create and they strive to achieve quality work and results, being happy to be accountable for the work being done.  When inspired, they are committed to success.  This creates a ripple effect that continues to inspire all involved.

When we work smart, we collaborate, we build partnerships, we increase productivity and we deliver quality solutions for our clients. This allows us to produce exceptional results for our clients.

Our professional consulting careers can ultimately take us anywhere. We will find ourselves taking on projects in other countries and continents. Our advanced knowledge in processes, technologies, marketing and more enable us to help our clients see and grasp a better world for themselves.

Consultants can be found providing services in many disciplines such as Marketing, Business and Finance, Information Technology, Environmental Studies, Human resources, Travel and Leisure, Retail and Online Selling, Manufacturing, Distribution, Public Sector, Telecommunications, High-tech, and more.

But through all these disciplines or fields of service, our goal is always to help our clients achieve sustainable improvements. We strive to create strategies that will help our clients achieve their business objectives, help transform them in some capacity and improve their futures.

We endeavor to build long-term relationships with our clients and we take these relationships seriously. We want to be their counselors and advisers over time. We work to stay with them to help them succeed over the longer term. We won't be needed every day, but we will be there when they need us.

When we are done, our clients are our friends and our evangelists...

# WHAT IT TAKES TO BE A CONSULTANT

There are a number of levels to consulting; everything from offering services of manual labour through to providing business or technological skills and intellectual effort to corporations. The common thread in this is that you have to market your services, sell the project and negotiate terms for its completion, complete the project, and last but not least, get paid. With my experience being in business and information technology consulting, my discussion herein will focus on that level of enterprise.

So what is a consultant and what does a consultant do?

• A consultant hires him/herself out to businesses/corporations for fixed or variable periods of time to perform a service needed by that business entity.
• A consultant, in most instances, will be at a completely arms-length business distance from the client corporation and will therefore not receive any benefits from the corporation that an employee would (medical, dental, holiday pay, etc.).
• A consultant usually must pay for all equipment, tools, computer equipment, supplies, and software that he or she needs to utilize while on the consulting engagement.
• All costs related to getting to the client location to complete the consulting engagement are usually borne by the consultant unless otherwise negotiated with the client prior to the engagement commencing.

- A consultant is often an individual proprietorship or "one person/small business" corporation.
- To work, a consultant needs to find each new client and secure a consulting contract for each engagement.
- A consultant when working, usually submits periodic invoices to the client (bi-weekly, semi-monthly or monthly) and then must wait to be paid by the client based on the payment terms defined in the client/consultant agreement/contract

What does it actually take then to become a successful consultant? First you have to put in the time to learn how to find and sell yourself on projects. This can take years depending on the discipline chosen. To be successful, you will then need:

- The Education – For Example, At Minimum, a College Degree to be Able to Cross Borders to Consult in Other Countries (E.g., Trade NAFTA Status – for USA and Canada cross border consulting projects or;
- You work as an affiliated representative of a consulting company allowed to complete projects in the target country or "state/Province" of that country – they would handle your cross border qualification
- The Resume – to Document Your Experience Levels to Prospective Clients
- Probably a Portable Computer and Your Own "Toolkit" of Current Project Delivery Applications, Templates, Agreements, Proposal Examples, Deliverable Examples, etc.

- Usable References – They Will Call Them!
- Access to and posting your resume and/or qualifications to several field related "Staffing/Resourcing Databases and Bulletin Boards"

Being a Consultant requires learning how to find clients for your services including learning how to:

- Leverage existing contacts to sniff out new project opportunities
- Use project resourcing bulletin boards
- Work LinkedIn, Google Plus and Facebook
- Utilize "Project Head-hunters"
- Collaborate with major consulting firms
- Build your CV, Skills Matrix and Usable Reference List
- Build quality proposal templates, Request for Information (RFI) templates, etc.
- Create agreement templates, travel & expense templates, non-disclosure agreements
- Build "Trade NAFTA" and other acceptable cross-border documentation for international opportunities
- Negotiate contracts with client prospects

As a consultant, you have the freedom to work for whoever you want and do whatever project you want – and this keeps life exciting. But remember, as a consultant, you must take care to ensure you get paid – you do not have the same safety nets that an employee has – such as Labour Boards, etc. Consulting can be very financially rewarding – but remember, every time you finish an engagement, you are in effect once again unemployed and looking for your next project. Can be stressful for some...but exiting for others.

# CONSULTING CERTIFICATIONS

Consulting is also about continuous learning. As you consult, you will be regularly in conversations with clients and client staff who are knowledgeable in their fields and probably read the same trade journals, magazines, online articles, etc. that you can. As a consultant, you have to maintain your credibility with them so you will need to stay at the top of your game which makes continuous learning a requirement so make this a part of every day. Read at least one thing related to your industry and profession every day – stay sharp to maintain your credibility with those you consult to.

Secondly, certifications also build your credibility, show you have done the work, and help you get consulting engagements. Every industry and profession has courses and certifications you can get that potential employers ask for – get them – they will earn you money!

Overall if you are doing management consulting, there is the Institute of Management Consultants certification in the USA and the Certified Management Consultant certification in Canada. This is very good to have but will take a few years to get – you can get some course exemptions for University classes taken which can shorten the program for you when you apply.

Every large consulting organization you will be competing against put their people through it and some clients won't let you get through the door to consult unless you have this certification or are at least enrolled in the program and show the enrollment on your resume.

In the technology and project management professions, there are also a number of certifications and diplomas you can get and any you do get, be sure to put on your resume and on the bulletin boards where you document your bio. These become keyword searches recruiters look for when they are trying to find resources for engagements. Just read a few resource required notices on Dice put out by recruiters and you will see what I mean.

There are many certifications out there you can get. For instance, if you are working to integrate financial systems applications for clients, you can get certifications for such applications as SAP, Oracle Financials and JD Edwards.

If you are a Business Process Re-engineering or organizational efficiency expert, strive to become a Baldridge Examiner or get certified for Six Sigma.

Microsoft has over 100 certificate courses that they offer and full programs such as the MCSE (Microsoft Certified Systems Engineer) program that you can take a series of courses in and complete – and resourcers do look for this one on a resume if you are an IT professional.

The big one in HR is the CHRP certification – Certified Human Resource Professional.

In the financial world, its the Chartered Accountant and Certified Management Accountant designations to go after.

So there are a number of certifications out there that will help you to be a recognized professional and these will help you in your consulting career. Do not stop learning and building your resume. Over time, you will be able to command the higher chargeout rates if you do.

# INCORPORATION OR PROPRIETORSHIP?

As people start their own business enterprises, they are often questioning whether or not they should be incorporating or should start operating as a proprietorship. Perhaps the information I provide in this chapter will help in this decision process.

First off, a proprietorship is the cheapest way to start a business. When you incorporate, expect to pay at least $1,000.00 or so to get that job done properly so right away, you have spent an additional $1,000.00 out of your start-up funds.

To operate as a proprietorship when starting out, you just have to register it with local government (and only if you operate under a business name instead of your own name in some jurisdictions – you will have to check this) agencies for little or no cost if it is required. If you are going to operate a brick and mortar location for example, a local business license would often be required but if you are just working in your home running an online business only without customers coming to your door, you most likely do not have to register with any government entity at all. Below are some additional advantages proprietorships have.

• Accounting is much simpler and therefore more inexpensive.
• It takes less working capital to go into business and you can start more quickly.

- If your business has a net loss, you can deduct the loss against employment income in your personal return.
- All revenues and profits go directly to you.
- Proprietorships have the lowest amount of regulatory burden/reporting. Corporations due to their increased sophistication (Directors, Shareholders, etc.) have more complex reporting requirements
- Corporations have to file "Annual Returns" – for "Good Standing", for "Taxation", payroll, GST submissions, Employer CPP and EI reporting, pension reporting, etc.
- Operating as a proprietorship, you can save some money on not having to pay Employer shares of CPP and E.I. payments – a deduction requirement if you are taking a salary of a corporation.

Proprietorship disadvantages include but are not limited to the following:

- Unlimited Liability – If things go wrong, you are exposed – any lawsuit can also go after your personal assets as well as the business assets.
- Proprietorships have a more difficult time arranging 3rd party financing and investment capital if some is needed. Corporations can issue stock…
- Corporations can elect to go public at some time in the future. A proprietorship needs to become a corporation before doing this.
- Income is taxed at your personal rate of tax which is higher than corporate tax rates. As your income increases as a proprietorship, you will be

paying more taxes on your earnings than a corporation would.

- A corporate business name, once established, is protected. No such strength of security of name with a proprietorship.

Corporations have the following advantages over proprietorships:

- Limited liability of Directors and Officers of the corporation in most instances
- Separate legal entity – Business name is also protected
- Easier to raise capital and more mechanisms available to do it – including shares and "classes of shares" (common, preferred, voting, non-voting, etc.)
- Ownership of a corporation is easily transferable and more easily saleable.
- The life of a corporation continues beyond the death of the original person creating the entity.
- Corporations can issue dividends to stakeholders – this can create significant tax breaks for the individuals receiving these tax breaks when they accept these dividends. They pay much less tax than if they were taking a salary from the corporation.

Some corporation disadvantages include:

- Extensive financial record keeping is required
- Corporations are closely regulated by government agencies

- Tax returns are more complex to complete – and now you have two returns to complete – a corporate return and a personal return...
- Business losses can't be written off against shareholder incomes (as in the case of a proprietorship)
- More complex to operate – you now have to define shareholders, directors and officers, classes of shares to be issued, etc. and report on these annually.

Some thoughts that I have about this topic in summary include the following:

- If you are in a business of low financial risk and possible lawsuits from outside parties, there is less pressure for you to incorporate. One reason people incorporate is to set up the second legal entity to limit personal financial exposure if things go wrong.
- Another reason for incorporation is in the instance where incomes and profits are becoming significant, enough so that you want the lower tax rates and incentives that are available to corporations and not to proprietorships and this has become more important than the increased work of maintaining an incorporated business entity.
- A third reason for incorporation is if there are multiple stakeholders involved in the venture and/or the venture is becoming large enough that it is looking to raise additional capital – often done through the issuance and offering of shares in the business entity.

• Corporations more easily survive the death of the initiator of the business. It is easier to pass your share of the corporation to others in your will.

In closing, individuals usually start out as proprietorships and evolve to become corporations as their businesses grow. If you have partners in the business, consider becoming a Limited Liability Partnership to minimize your personal financial exposure.

If you become a one person or small corporation, consider taking dividends as opposed to salaries in the corporation.

If the first year or two of the business will show losses (Initial investment costs, few customers, etc.), and you still are earning employment income as well, consider remaining a Proprietorship so you can offset these losses against your employment income in your personal tax return.

# THE PROS AND CONS TO BEING A CONSULTANT

You are probably an employed person frustrated with trying to get ahead financially and you are thinking there must be a better way to earn more and keep more of the money you do earn so in the back of your mind, you think a career as a consultant may be more rewarding – I was thinking this too once many years ago. Truth is; it can be extremely rewarding although I didn't know that when I started out but I had just stumbled onto one elemental truth that changed my world.

Reading a "Rich Man Poor Man" book one day, I realized that on salary, you make "X" dollars and then pay tax on it and that as a self-employed person, you make "X" dollars then you deduct any related business expenses, then you pay a similar tax percentage on the net of your income less these related expenses. Once I realized that this included the costs of my vehicle to get to the project, depreciation on said vehicle, and a portion of my at home costs (rent, mortgage, utilities, phone, etc.) to operate my business out of my home; I was sold. Not only could I earn a higher rate of pay for my time (Consultants generally make more per hour than employees), but I could net out all these costs of doing business and then just pay my taxes on the remainder – ultimately, a significantly lesser amount of actual tax paid than an employee had to pay.

So this was my primary motivation for ultimately becoming a consultant: You make more gross revenues and you pay less total tax on it. If you can keep busy, this can be a very rewarding way to live your life – and it theoretically can set you up for a comfortable retirement. This is a simple formula for making good money – but there is one catch: You have to market yourself to get busy again once you complete a project and there is no guarantee that you will find your next project when you want to!

This stops a lot of people from doing this. The security of the pay cheque and possibility of the pension at the end of it keeps them handcuffed to their jobs even if they don't like their jobs. Of course there is another reality, many people just don't have the drive and strength to regularly market themselves, the experience or the knowhow to complete projects for others successfully, or even enough understanding as to how to get started doing this – and the fear of not knowing enough can be debilitating to many. Taking a risky jump into a world you don't understand when you have bills to pay each month and when you may have others to take care of that depend on you, is a frightening thing to do.

Consulting is not the answer to everyone but the key point I am trying to make here is don't just back away from doing it because these fears are holding you back. You will never make more than just a highly taxed salary if you don't do something like this in life so you will work your years away possibly at jobs you don't enjoy for the sake of the pay cheque and supporting your family and you will run the risk of reaching your retirement years with very little set aside to retire with unless there is a good company pension waiting for you.  It is my belief that for many, you owe it to yourself to at least research what it takes to be a successful consultant and then to honestly assess yourself as to whether or not you think you have enough to offer to potential clients to succeed.  Don't decide not to risk due to ignorance or fear only. If you decide not to risk it, let it be because you have honestly analyzed the pros and cons and the risks and rewards of it first.  If you try it and fail, well, you can always go out and find another job.

I for one have found my life as a consultant to be an extremely rich experience and a financially rewarding one.  I am nearing retirement age now in significantly much better financial shape than I believe I would have reached it as an employee and as a bonus, I have had a lifetime of travel and of completing extremely exciting projects all over the world. I would not have traded my consulting and resulting life experiences for anything else – for me, it has been a wonderful ride.  It might be for you as well – so research it and consider it.

## FINDING YOUR NICHE AS A CONSULTANT

There are any number of people who dream of leaving their employee work lives and dream of becoming a consultant of some sort. So, to assist these people in their dreams, I'd like to share what I have seen over the years (being a consultant myself) as to some of the more common "consulting niches" or "disciplines" that one can pursue. This list includes the following:

Business Consulting
- Business Strategic Planning
- Business Roll Out Planning / Strategy Development
- Business Process Design and Business Process Re-Engineering
- Business Performance Consulting – KPI Metrics Development and Measurement, ISO Certifications, Six Sigma, etc.
- Business Disruption Planning / Disaster Recovery Planning
- Product Planning, Product Design, Product Rollout Planning
- Financial Planning, Raising Capital, Investment Planning
- Going Public Consulting

Information Technology
- Programming Core Application Systems
- Website Development

- Graphic Art – Website and Social Media (Images, Videos, Logos, Products, etc.)
- Network and Device Management and Support
- Database Development, Management and Support
- Interface Development and 3$^{rd}$ Party Interface Development
- Data Warehousing, Data Mining and KPI/Statistical Report Development
- Strategic Planning and Architecture Strategy Development (Application Systems, Infrastructure, Performance, etc.)

Financial Consulting
- Outsourced/In-sourced Book-Keeping Services
- Tax Consulting
- Government Grant Consulting, Preparation and Submission (SR&ED Grants, etc.)
- Payroll Management, Accounts Payable, Accounts Receivable and Banking

Marketing Consulting
- Marketing Plan Development
- Advertising Development (Direction Planning, Budgeting, Partner Definition and Contracting, Target Market Definition and Profiling, etc.)
- Advertisement Creation (Adds, Videos, News Items, Store Displays, Website Displays, Social Media, etc.)
- Product Preparation (Packaging, Labelling, User Guides, Pricing Research and Pricing, etc.)

Human Resource Consulting
- Organizational Planning (Business Structures, Resource Structure Definition, Span of Control Definition, etc.)
- Resource/Skills Definition, Responsibility Matrices, and Requirements Planning
- Staffing and Recruitment, Background Checks, Job Board Postings, etc.
- Labour Relations, Contract Negotiations, etc.
- Benefits and Compensation Planning
- Performance Monitoring, Salary/Wage Management, Recognition and Rewards
- Conflict Management and Resolution, Human Rights Violations, etc.

Travel Consulting
- Trip Booking and Trip/Itinerary Management
- Flight, Cruise, Hotel and Car Rental Bookings
- Wardrobe Consulting
- Destination Planning
- Travel Brochure Creation, Custom Destination Package Creation
- Passport and Travel Document Preparation and Submission
- Lodging and Accommodation Services
- Tour Development, Marketing and Management
- Trip, Timeshare, Cruise, etc. - Telephone Marketing Sales Affiliates

In summary, your life earned skills will lead you down viable paths to begin your consulting career. Before embarking on it however, be sure to prepare for it by creating whatever you might need in terms of templates such as proposals, non-disclosure agreements, checklists, tools, deliverables, etc. The more you have readied beforehand, the better the quality of the deliverables you can create for your clients and the less strain it will be on you to create them, particularly if you are under time constraints to get things to a client or potential client.

Know your markets and target clients and understand beforehand how much you can charge for an hourly rate for what you do and how much you can charge for travel and related expenses. Always try to negotiate travel expenses into your contract where you can. If you can't build it in as a visible component to the negotiated agreement, build it into your charge-out hourly or day rate to the client so you don't end up working too cheaply.

Seek some form of up front retainer for expenses where possible if it is out of town work. It is a lot easier to be exposed on your spent time than on actual expenses you have had to pay for on your credit cards if the client doesn't pay you. Build this into your contract if you feel it to be necessary and don't get on site until you have this money.

Some paths may allow you to start out slowly or part-time and it might be advantageous to complete the first engagement or two while you still have a salaried position if you can as consulting is not ultimately for everyone. Lastly, remember that a consultant, when they walk onto a client's site, is usually expected to know more than most of the internal employees do about your chosen area of expertise!

Trade NAFTA (North American Free Trade Agreement), written into law many years ago, allows professional consultants to work in each others countries (Canada, USA and Mexico) with minimal cross border paperwork to be completed. For Canadians, if you have the correct documentation along with $50.00 US with you as you reach a USA border crossing; you will be passed right through. Note: Be sure to have the exact amount with you – border officials do not give change.

When you cross, you will receive a "TN" card that you need to carry with you in your passport while abroad. This is a repeat entry card good for up to one year for the client you are contracted to so if a Canadian border official tries to take it from you on your return, be sure to tell him this is a re-entry situation and you will be going back down to consult to the same client again. They have to then give the card back to you. If you let them have it, you will have to get approved all over again on your next trip south. Note: Even with this card in hand, you will need to return to Canada at least once every six months – even if only for a weekend.

Note that your family can come with you to the USA but they are not allowed to seek employment there. They cross as normal tourists and need no paperwork to cross if they are Canadian citizens. There are also a few banking considerations you need to be aware of. For example:

- A US dollar cheque from a Canadian bank account often is not cashable when presented in a US bank for payment (Issues with ACH clearing transactions) – vice versa usually an issue as well. Clearing a foreign cheque is at the discretion of the bank involved and it is a headache for them to process the transaction so they will often just not do it.

- If they do process it, be aware that they could put a hold on the cheque for a considerable amount of time – could take as long as 30 days before you get access to those funds.

- Under Trade NAFTA as a consultant, you can get a "limited - TN" U.S. social security card and number that will allow you to open a US bank account. Therefore, if you are a Canadian receiving US checks from American clients, you can accept these cheques and can deposit them in a US Bank Account you have set up for this purpose.

- Lastly, a few Canadian banks do have agreements in place with certain banks in the USA so you can clear cheques cross border – you will need to research this on a bank by bank basis.

Some Tax Information Relating to Getting Paid in the USA

- Under a B2B contract, a USA employer may request that you as the contractor have a USA issued corporation E.I.N. number and a USA Bank account set up. Under this structure, you might have to find a US consulting corporation to go through to work for this client, and they may require a percentage of your rate in order to handle the processing and billing work around your project. Be careful to ensure that your "TN" status stays clean through whatever structure you ultimately set up. It has to be clear to the immigration officials who your client is, that you are coming from Canada to consult to that US based client and that you, the Canadian will be getting paid by that client. This may mean in certain circumstances that your client becomes the go between consulting organization.

- Under a B2-Consultant, "TN" contract, if the client company agrees to retain you under a "TN" status contract, you will need to complete a 1040NR and an 8840 form. Then you just get a W-2 from the client for the work performed in the US that year and that makes filing your tax forms very easy in Canada. You will convert the amount received into Canadian dollars and then you claim a foreign tax credit in your Canadian return using the appropriate schedules to the T1.

In closing, cross border consulting can be very lucrative for Canadians, especially with favourable currency conversion rates in effect such as they now are. You will most likely require at a minimum a college level degree in place and a minimum of around 5 years of consulting experience in your area of expertise to be allowed across the border to consult under the Trade NAFTA agreement terms.

To get your "TN" card, you will require a letter from your client in the other country requesting your assistance as part of your package. Be sure to specifically mention your expertise as one of the categories found in Appendix 1602.D.1 of the NAFTA agreement. I once listed my trade as "Computer Systems Architect" instead of "Computer Systems Analyst" and got turned back at the border crossing. Use their exact terminology!

You will find that there is paperwork to deal with, but it is not insurmountable – just a little complicated. By the way, there is some new legislation relating to "TN" related accounting currently being contemplated in the USA – so do keep watching the news on this – as the full effects of this are still to be understood.

Best of luck with your cross border consulting plans.

# A FEW THOUGHTS ON BUSINESS PROCESS RE-ENGINEERING

Business Process Re-Engineering (BPR) in its truest form should always take a top down approach to ensure its efforts are in full alignment with the core vision for the corporation, it's core values, it's overall desired business model and the core purpose and tasks that the corporation needs to perform well to deliver the products, services and value to its customers that help it to be successful and profitable. True, often targeted BPR efforts take place deep within a corporation where only small subsets of it are being re-architected, but knowledge of the above visions, values and models should never be lost sight of even in a targeted effort.

Following are several guiding "Principles" or "Best Practices" that have given me practical guidelines to use with clients when undertaking process re-engineering projects. A couple are mine and a few are from others such as Mike Hammer in his 1994 book "Re-Engineering the Corporation". Keeping people cognizant of these Principles throughout a BPR effort can help keep your process facilitation workshops with a client on track. Just point to these principles when you see a person with a "personal stakes or agenda" trying to take you off on a tangent due to personal interests. It helps bring them back into alignment.

- We will develop new processes in alignment with the Business Vision and the core tasks of the corporation rather than trying to fix existing processes.
- Business Process Re-engineering will be done in partnership with business, application, and technology personnel to ensure the best possible results.
- We will not place constraints on the definition of the problem nor the scope of the re-engineering effort. The focus will be on complete process streams, not organizational departments.
- We will not allow existing corporate cultures and management attitudes to interfere with finding the best possible solutions for the organization as a whole.
- A professional with the required skillset will lead each process design effort.
- We will not pull back when we encounter resistance and will not settle for just marginal improvements in processes.
- We will remember that the "Needs of the many outweigh the needs of the few, or the one". (Borrowed from a Star Trek Movie – but I loved its applicability to BPR!)

As you facilitate, there are a few concepts to keep in mind as you work your way through these workshop sessions:

- Avoid getting too detailed too quickly. Work at a high level initially and then gradually drill down into greater levels of detail.
- Follow the 80/20 rule. Concentrate on the processes and applications that affect 80% of the people first and only tackle the other 20% if there is time.
- Define a gap as "Anything the vanilla software doesn't do". If the process can't change, add it to the

gap list and move on to the next process or functionality requirement. Don't get bogged down trying to solve the gap.

- Don't get stuck on the idea of "But that's how we do it now". Be open minded to new approaches.

High level often found process categories resident within a corporation could include the following.

**Strategic Business Processes:** These processes deliver value to the organization in terms of using history and other management information to make key strategic decisions. Four core business process types often include the following:

- Leadership Processes
- Strategic Planning
- People and Process Effectiveness
- Manage Alliance Partners and Stakeholders

**Core Tasks:** These are the direct tasks or processes that deliver value to customers and stakeholders. Common core tasks might include:

- Design Products
- Develop Products
- Market Products
- Sell Products
- Assemble Products – Integrated Supply Chain + Factory Activities
- Transport Products – Logistics
- Service and Support Products

**Support Processes:** These processes provide indirect support, yet are no less important, to the delivery of core value to customers and stakeholders and could include the following:

- Financial Stewardship

- Human Resources
- Environment & Safety
- Contracts Management
- Public Relations and Communications
- Facilities Engineering
- Maintenance
- Legal & Insurance
- Records Management

In general, all processes having direct contact with the customer and/or forming part of the value creation chain for the customer can be viewed as being **external** processes. As these activities are the main interface with the customer, they should be developed and guided to ensure the maximum level of empowerment to enable staff to get as close to the customer as possible to fulfill the customer requirement on first contact.  This assumes that employees are supported by the appropriate level of automation and training within a solid framework of policies to allow transactions and interactions to be handled within an adequately controlled environment.

The processes that create value for the organization by enabling control, planning, management, etc. may be seen as being **internal** processes. These are less geographically dependent on customer location and can be located wherever makes logical sense.

For those initiating efforts to improve the way their organization does business, I hope these few principles and guidelines will help you to be more successful consulting to them.

## INTRODUCTION TO FINDING CLIENTS AND SECURING ENGAGEMENTS

Think back to a time when you were laid off from or had quit a job and were forced to again look for work. You start thinking about what you want to do next, what skills you might have that companies would pay for, what opportunities might exist in your area for you to find employment, you might even be filling out forms to get government payments while unemployed. This may happen to you maybe once or only a few times in your life and it can be stressful.

This happens to consultants a few to several times a year. In fact, it is actually a component of the day to day existence of a consultant. Even while still employed by a client, a consultant is often found looking for his or her next project or is looking for an additional project he or she might even be able to complete while still working for the current client. Being a consultant means, in effect, to be always looking for work. So you get quite good at it over time.

As you mature as a consultant, you actually start to build a daily looking for work routine that you employ to find your next "gig". You may turn this off some days or for periods of time during particularly long engagements, but you will usually still be doing parts of this routine to keep your "network" alive and to keep others thinking about you, keeping your name in their minds. Should something come up that your skills might be suited for, you want them thinking about you.

There are several key components to this "networking" process – and that is what consultants prefer to call it as opposed to job or project hunting by the way. This part of the full 5-part consulting course drills down on these components to summarize for the student what he or she will be needing to do to find and secure future engagements.

Starting with finding opportunities and clients for future engagements, in overview, the consultant will likely be undertaking the following sorts of activities:

• Contacting previous clients to see if they have any new projects coming up that the consultant could assist with;

• Perusing "project bulletin boards" looking for larger scoped projects that the consultant might be able to become a part of;

• Contacting various "head-hunters" to let them know about your upcoming availability for work;

• Posting your resume and availability for work on "head-hunting" bulletin boards;

• Contacting various consulting organizations to build their awareness of you, your skills and your willingness to participate as a sub-contractor in one of their projects;

• Contacting other consultants that you have worked with in the past with a view to possibly collaborating together to undertake a larger scoped project as a team you put together for the specific engagement opportunity;

• Perusing news notices in industry trade daily or weekly magazines to see if anything is being posted there that might lead to a project opportunity

- Looking to see if there are any industry related trade shows occurring while the consultant is "between gigs" that he or she might attend with a view to both staying information current and to continue networking with attendees to the shows and with those running the "booths" at those events.
- Checking out various government project "bid" notification bulletin boards.
- Contacting friends made over the years who may know of some upcoming project where they might be employed.

Once opportunities are identified for projects, the nature of the project itself will determine how the consultant will work to try to become a part of it. These approaches will be discussed in more detail in another lecture in this series but in overview, it could entail as little as sending in a resume and your service chargeout rate to undertaking and spearheading the writing of a complete proposal, resourcing it, etc.

Often the first hurdle to overcome when trying to secure a competitive bid project is to make the project "short-list" which brings the consultant to another set of tasks that need to be undertaken in trying to wrestle the project away from the other short-listed candidates. This also will be covered in one of the lectures in this course.

Then you get to the project price, resourcing and final scoping activities to be done with a client before an engagement letter can be completed and signed off on by all parties and the project can commence.

Head Hunters, more politically correctly referred to as staffing recruiters or placement services, come to the professional consulting world from a few different directions and it's good to know which direction they are talking to you from when you are in project and rate discussions with them.

The first direction is that recruiters work to build long term relationships with corporations that do regular hiring for permanent and contract positions. In this capacity, they usually make their remuneration deals with said corporations and you as the project seeking professional will not have to worry about giving them a percentage of your project earnings when you are placed on the project. You just have to get through their screening process in order to get onto the short-list and make it to an interview with the employer to pass final inspection and negotiate your chargeout rates.

It is usually these types of recruiting organizations that place the adds on Dice and other bulletin boards on behalf of the corporations doing the hiring. You will see many of these projects posted by national recruiting agencies right alongside actual corporations placing their own adds for resources needed. On Dice, you are primarily looking to get staffed on pre-defined projects that are now ready for staffing and you as an independent are looking to fulfill one of the slots. This is not where you will be looking for complete projects to bid a team into.

Recruiters usually do the work of filtering out the applicants that adds engender and present short-lists of candidates to the employer Human Resource departments for final selections, job interviews, final rate and expenses negotiations, etc. The recruiter may negotiate with you on rates to a point, but their work in this regard is only to see if they can get you to commit to an initial number that is within the acceptable range parameters of what the employer is willing to pay for the resource.

This is part of their "short-listing" process by the way. If you hold out for too much money, you won't get presented to the corporation as a potential candidate for the role so it is a delicate dance that you have to do with the recruiter as you don't know what that contract rate range is and you want to get as high a number for your services as you can without losing your shot at the project. You will get better at this negotiation process over time – you just have to get through it a few times to improve your skills at it.

Another way that you will find yourself working with recruiters or recruiting agencies is directly. In this instance either you have contacted them or they have found you and they want to do the work to represent you to clients for a fee. If they have found you, they have either found your resume on a bulletin board somewhere (such as on Dice) or you have submitted a resume for something posted in the past through their organization and they have kept your resume on file in case something else came along that required your skill set.

Just so you know, on Dice and on any other similar bulletin board that hosts both candidate resumes and resourcing opportunities, there are people out there who make a living trolling these Boards trying to connect candidates and corporations needing services trying to place resources that they can make a percentage on. You as the commodity in the process irrespective of how or who is contacting you must work to preserve the best rate for yourself for an engagement because once you agree to something for a period of time, that is what you will earn for that foreseeable future time frame so don't sell yourself to short if you are a very skilled resource – others will be looking for you as well.

One last point to make about this is that getting resourced to a project this way reduces your earnings because you are now having to pay the middleman for your services. You can troll these bulletin boards yourself to find these same projects and cut out the middle man so you make more money. The more you are willing to do this type of work yourself, the higher your take home revenues will be.

There is one scenario though where it can make sense to work with one of these recruitment organizations. If this is a well established recruiter in a locality and they have well established relationships with local organizations and are trusted by them to bring to them top quality resources, you can register with them for placement on projects that they find because you know they will get you a project. Their name will help carry you in the front door. It will take you work to find out who these companies are though but they can become valuable to you once you find them in your locale.

A last point on this recruitment topic that it is important to understand. This relates to conflict of interest. Always be aware of exclusivity terms when working with recruiters. Be sure you really are who you want to be with if working with anyone directly and be careful of what you sign. Sometimes projects come up that some group wins and you could be a good resource to fill a slot within the project but you have previously aligned yourself under an exclusive placement deal with someone else. This will stop you from getting on a project that you might otherwise be well suited for. So be careful what kinds of deals you sign up for with recruiters and don't sign exclusivity deals unless you absolutely have to.

# WORKING AS AN INDEPENDENT WITH CONSULTING FIRMS

Consulting firms come in a couple of forms. The first of which are the large multi-national accounting and audit firms that also have built in additional consulting practices. They provide global consulting services to large corporations in a number of disciplines some examples of which include:

Business Strategy Related Engagements
Information Technology Consulting
Human Resource Consulting
Government Grant Development – Such as SR@ED
(Scientific Research and Experimental Development)
Forensic Accounting
Feasibility Studies
and much more

Some of the most well known of these types of organizations known as the Big Four, include the following:

Ernst & Young
Price Waterhouse Coopers
Deloitte Touche
KPMG Peat Marwick

Then there several very large focused consulting organizations some of the most well known including:

McKinsey & Company
The Boston Consulting Group
Bain & Company
Booz & Company

Deloitte Consulting
Monitor Group
Mercer LLC
Accenture
EDS

All of the above organizations operate globally so if you build relationships with them, you could end up on projects worldwide. You can also start searching for other national and regional consulting organizations to associate yourself with. An hour on Google and you'll be able to find a number of them consulting in geographies where you might wish to work.

Probably the biggest difference between working with recruiters for projects than in working with consulting firms is that of just being presented as an independent to fulfill a role on an existing project as to that of becoming part of a team being put together to propose some form of turn-key project.

The consulting firm will be looking to staff each of the roles they will be proposing on a project but the proposal will still have to go in to the potential employing corporation and the business in most instances will be a competitive bid situation and will still need to be won against other consulting groups making similar bids for the work.

Often, these competitive bid proposal efforts can take months to get closure on so you can start working whereas recruiters looking to place you on existing projects can often turn around the entire process to a point where you get hired within the span of a few days or a week.

So do not be looking for a quick turnaround to employment if you are trying to land a spot on one of these types of projects. A second thing to be aware of. Even if the consulting organization is successful in winning the project, you still may not be able to work on it. The primary reason for this is that they will always be trying to get their internal resources busy ahead of you the independent because they make more money that way.

A second point is this. When these types of proposals go in to a client for example, unless you are defined as a "Key Resource" who will be made available no matter what, most of these proposals go in with a clause that says something like this: "The consultants proposed within this bid are representative only. We will endeavor to make them available for this project but if they are found to be busy elsewhere at the time of project initiation, we will replace this consultant with another resource having similar or improved skills to fulfill the required project tasks."

These are the "weasel" words in a proposal that gives the consulting firm an out to replace one resource with another should a project bid be successful. They can also use this clause to oust you from the project if they want to use their own resource instead. Often called the "bait and switch" clause with clients, astute potential clients will force bidding consulting organizations to guarantee certain particular resources they liked from the proposal as a condition relating to contract acceptance.

So while it is good to have these relationships in place, you do have to be aware that they don't guarantee work for you on a project win. Naturally, the better your personal relationships with the actual people involved from the consulting organization, the stronger the likelihood that they will keep you involved when project wins occur.

Another benefit to being involved in these types of projects is that project success or failure primary liability rests with the consulting organization instead of you. If something goes wrong, they are on the hook for it much more than you. They also will be walking in with core credibility you don't have, methodologies and toolkits to use on the project that exceed what you may have that will help in the project being successful, and probably some very solid project managers or project oversight personnel that can help to ensure the project does not go off the rails.

The bottom line is that working on a few of these projects will be a good experience for you if you can manage to get a slot on one of them. You will learn a lot about professional consulting, approaches, frameworks, methodologies and more. It is well worth your time to build a few connections with these types of organizations to try and get a few of their engagements under your belt. And, it doesn't hurt your resume in the least to have a few "Fortune" level clients appearing on them.

## BUILDING A TEAM THAT CAN BE PROPOSED ON PROJECTS

As you progress through your business life and your consulting career, you will come across individuals whose work you like and who you just flat out enjoy working with you. Keep these people close to you and never lose touch with them. I have friendships I have built over the years that I have never lost and they are still just a call away if a project comes my way and I have an opportunity to propose a team to execute it.

One of things I have done is maintained a folder of these special people on my computer and I have made sure to stay in touch with them from time to time by phone, e-mail, Facebook and LinkedIn. Many times in my life, I have put together teams and have also participated in projects with these individuals and my life has been enriched because of it. Consulting can be fun with friends and friends with skills are a real bonus.

As you evolve in your consulting life, you build client relationships that can lead to additional projects over time delivered through teams that you can put together yourself. In effect, you become a small consulting company in your own right and you start to place resources on projects sometimes under people you trust or under your direct management.

There will be times that you have to reach out beyond those you personally know and have available in order to respond to requests for proposals to complete project engagements. Well guess what, you can go to exactly the same places that recruiters go to get resources. Put adds out there on Dice and other bulletin boards, receive resumes from interested parties, interview and select candidates and put your own projects together.

There are no real rules to this. Go with what you feel you need to do, make deals that you are comfortable making with these resources being sure to protect yourself in the process, and get those proposals in. If it is your opportunity and your proposal you have every right to take a bit off the top for each resource you find and propose on a project. My usually override on placing these resources has always been around 20%. It covers my costs and protects me financially to a point and it also maximizes what I pay to those who are happy to get working again. By paying them at the 80% level, I usually get future loyalty from them on projects as this is more than they can usually get from head hunting organizations.

Prior to submitting your proposal to the client, do what you can to get confirmations from all your team members that they will participate in the project if the client OK is given within a certain amount of time – remember that you can't expect them to stay sitting on the bench waiting for your OK call for too long. They have make money too. I usually create a confirmation e-mail or letter to my team members prior to proposal submission that I ask them to respond to or sign and get back to me prior to proposal submission. My bench strength is not that of a major consulting firm so the fewer resources surprises the better.

As you do this more and more, you start to build a good collection of resumes. Remember to politely contact those you couldn't immediately fit into the project you were going after but who had submitted resumes to you. Let them know that you will keep them in mind for other engagements you are going after as well and ask them if you can continue to propose them on potential projects subject to their final approval in each instance. In this way, you become a small consulting company yourself over time with some internal "bench strength" that you don't have to pay. Stay in contact with this team from time to time – setup a team newsletter, encourage inter-team communications, etc. as they can also bring you opportunities for you're your collective team to propose on. Stay fluid with them on terms as these will all be consulting professionals in their own right and you want to be treating them in effect, as equals on the ventures you go after. Only take "spin" on them where it is earned and warranted. Treat them right and they'll treat you right.

# RESPONDING TO AN RFP – REQUEST FOR PROPOSAL

Responding to a Request for Proposal is a totally different method of trying to get work than most people ever face in their lives. When you are looking for a job, you phone around, send in resumes, follow up and try to get hired if there appears to be interest in you. As an independent contractor trying to get a consulting gig, you are most likely getting your engagement in a similar manner. You work through or with a head-hunter or potential employer, you send in your resume and desired consulting rates, you follow up and you try to get hired if they express an interest.

Responding to an RFP to get work is entirely different. First, you have to be known as a serious consulting business in order to get invited to respond in the first place or you are registered on a public sector database somewhere that allows you to respond, or the potential employer knows you for some reason beforehand and invites you to respond. It is usually a relatively closed circle of respondees that are allowed to respond to any RFP bid but out by a potential employing business entity.

When an RFP is offered for response, there are usually a few formal steps that the Consultant will be going through as part of the official process viewable by the potential employer. These would include:

• Sending in a formal response letter that you intend to respond to the RFP before the defined deadline.

- There is usually an opportunity to submit additional questions you might have about the RFP after you have had a chance to read the RFP document. These questions often have a due date of their own for submission when a formal RFP process is occurring.
- The potential employer then has the option of publishing the questions and their answers publically to all RFP respondees so you often have to be careful as to what questions you ask because you do not want to give away any of your gleaned insights to the project to any of the others bidding for the work; or,
- The potential employer may also wish to hold an open question and answer forum instead. All potential respondees are invited to attend and your questions are asked in an open session.
- Most often, to preserve impartiality, the Consultant's access to the client is restricted while the competitive bid process is being undertaken. Even if the potential client personnel evaluating the bids are close friends, you best move is to not approach them as this could lead to conflict of interest perceptions or situations and you may be asked to withdraw from the bid process so you will need to be careful while the process is on.

Getting to the response itself, it is not uncommon that to provide a comprehensive response that will be able to address all that the client is asking for to have completed, a collaboration between more than one consulting entity is required. In these instances, the consulting entities involved in the collective bid will decide among themselves which of them will be the "Prime" respondent and which will be sub-contractors to the bid being submitted.

The "Prime" will then conduct all formal discussions and negotiations with the potential client and will also be responsible for the final contract agreement and ultimate project delivery. Sub-contractors to the agreement will then negotiate their own services contracts with the "Prime" prior to Proposal submission so the "Prime" can represent them to the target employer.

As to the RFP response / Proposal itself, the proposal response will have a "shelf-life" – i.e., will remain active for a certain period of time and will become null and void after the defined end date expires. This is done to protect all parties involved.

The potential employer usually reviews the proposals for a period of time (usually defined in the initial RFP document) and then announces a list of short-listed candidates. After the short-listed candidates are announced, more information about the upcoming project may be revealed to these candidates, clarifications made on items that may have been previously misunderstood by respondees, an additional meeting or meetings may occur between client and respondees and the Consultants often will have one more opportunity to create a "Best and Final" offer for the project which they can present utilizing the additional information they have subsequently learned about it.

After reviewing the Best and Finals, the client will select and announce a Bid winner and the process is complete except for the next steps to be undertaken between the Client and the Consultant. These steps normally include:

- Going through the winning proposal in detail to finalize all terms within it and tasks to be completed
- Finalizing the Consultant project delivery team
- Finalizing the Client project team and acceptors
- Finalizing the project location, space allocations for the Consultants, support materials and technologies to be provided by the Client, etc.
- Project start date, payment terms, etc.
- Project scope of work and initial project plans
- Creation of the Project Engagement Letter and its signoff by both parties

On signoff of the engagement letter, the project is ready to commence and both sides move forward to start putting everything in place to start work.

# THE ART OF PROPOSAL WRITING

Writing a good proposal really is an art form. As technical or as boring as the base content within it might be from a pure reading perspective, you need to do everything you can to make the proposal flow and read well to continue to grab the attention of the reader. You also have to sell yourself and your business entity at the same time.

So you have to catch their attention, you have to keep their attention and you have to, as they read your content, become believers in you that if they hire you, you will get the job done, you won't waste their money and that they will never look to their bosses within the company like they made a mistake by hiring the wrong consulting organization to assist them.

This takes work and it takes polish. Whatever the amount of time you have between receiving the invitation to send in a proposal and the deadline imposed to get it into the hands of the customer, use it to go through your proposal over and over again, tweaking it, improving verbiage, moving things around so it flows better, improving the presentation of provided resumes, your corporate qualifications, etc.

You won't win every competition you write a proposal for, but you want to be in there doing the best work you can every time. Your corporate reputation rides with this.

And you just never know what might happen. I remember losing a bid once due to price when another contractor low balled it, but then I was approached and my team was brought in part way through the engagement being undertaken by the winner because they were messing up the delivery. When I asked why we were chosen, the Client said that ours had been the best proposal they had remembered reading but that they went the other way to try to save money on the project.

So now to get to the writing of the proposal itself. You will doubtless over time build your own templates for the proposals you write for your own consulting niche and the more you work at this, the better your templates will become.

When responding to public sector RFP's and a few private sector entities however, they will often push you into a certain standardized response design of their own choosing as this makes it easier for them to review and compare responses. When these situations occur, just do the best you can. You will find yourself doing a lot of copying and pasting from your template into their formats but you'll just have to work your way through it.

When you can use your own template, you are much more free to go with your own template designs. You can even build in links to additional promotional content you may have built that can enhance your corporate image – such as promotional videos you may have created on YouTube for example or selected pages on your business website.

Following is a table of contents that you might desire to use as a starting point for building your own styled proposal templates. Feel free to modify this to your own style as you see fit.

**Cover Page** – Describes the key project particulars such as who the Client is, who the Consultant is, the Project Name, Project Start Date, Reference Number if Required, Proposal Date, etc.

**Table of Contents** – Provides the detailed table of contents for all proposal sections.

**Executive Summary** – Builds in overview a summary of the situation and the details of the proposal. It is not unusual for proposals to reach or exceed 50 pages so often, you would want to put the key information the Client would be looking for in this Executive Summary as many Client executives would not want to have to read the entire document.

Often, you put into this summary, things like an overview of what the project is to be, when it starts, expected duration, key resources and assumptions and estimated total project costs.

**Our Understanding of Your Current Situation** – This is usually a reworking of what the Client has told you about the project rephrased in your words to show you understand what they want and to frame up how your methodology or approach to the project will provide them with the solution they want.

**Our Solution Methodology** – Here you spell out in more detail the approach steps you will be taking to complete the project for them.

**Our Team's Project Roles and Responsibilities** – This section documents each consultant's name, the roles they will play on the project (such as Project Manager, lead Architect, Application Architect, Database Architect, Business Analyst, etc.) and what their responsibilities will be to assist you the Client in achieving project success.

**Your Project Team's Required Roles for Project Success** – Here you document what you will need from the Client in terms of available resources and the roles they will need to fulfill to ensure project success.

**Project Timelines, Resourcing, Tasks and Costs** – Here you provide your initial High Level Project Plan for the project, the anticipated amount of effort each high level task will take to complete, which consultant will complete it, what the consultant's chargeout rate is and an estimate for their total cost to the project including Contingency estimates.

**Our Qualifications** – This section is used to promote yourself as a professional organization capable of undertaking this project for the Client. Here you can reference prior similar successful engagements completed for other clients, the size and scope of your enterprise, how you are able to bring in uniquely skilled professionals to perform top quality work for the Client, etc.

**Our References** – Most Client's will usually ask for some references they can call both corporate and for the individual consultants that will be used on this project. It is a good idea for you the consultant to always have in your toolkit a list such as this where you have companies, names and numbers that can be used and you have previously contacted these people to ensure they are willing to be called as a reference for work you have done for them in the past.

**Appendix A: Biographies / Resumes of Team Members** – At the end of your proposal, provide the biographies or resumes of the consultants you will be using on the project. Please note that the more you can standardize the format for each consultant to be used, the more they will look like a part of your permanent team as opposed to just being someone they grabbed from a bulleting board advertisement. This helps your cause as it gives the Client more comfort that each of these resources is familiar with your project methodology so the team will be more cohesive on site, knowing what to do and able to hit the ground running when they start spending the Client's money.

This should give you some idea as to how you need to spend time to build your proposal templates in advance of a project so that you can craft them into a professional looking document beforehand. Having to do all this on the fly after a Client asks for a proposal will otherwise set you up for several very sleepless nights as you try to get the job done and looking professional

# BUILDING THE INITIAL SCOPE OF WORK (SOW)

The Scope of Work also referred to as the Statement of Work (SOW) within a proposal bid, provides a summary of the work effort that is to be completed within the defined project. This section of a proposal provides a framework for what is to be included in the work effort and just as importantly, what is to be excluded.

This is one of the most critical components of a proposal to be accurate on as there have been numerous incidences within the sphere of contracted for services where a Client when a project is nearing completion has a different expectation as to what will be delivered than what the Consultant believes is to be delivered.

These differences of viewpoint have led to project disputes, project cancellations and even the occasional lawsuit between parties. If there is one thing in a proposal to take the time to define accurately, this is it.

Let's talk about the two types of proposals that a consultant might write. One that is a response to an RFP and one that is freely submitted upon an informal request by a potential client.

In a formal RFP situation, it is to a point incumbent on the Client to define within the RFP document enough clarity to what the Scope of Work is that the Consultant will be bidding on. The issue arises with this approach is that the Client is usually trying to define what the problem is and my not fully understand what the underlying root causes of the problem are when they are writing the RFP document.

They know they have a problem, they think they know what is causing it, but they may not be certain which is one of the reasons they are asking for consulting help in the first place.

As you write your proposal in response to an RFP document, you will take all the information provided in that document and will build your proposal based on what it tells you. However, you know that you are receiving only partial information and assumptions you make about what tasks you will have to perform during the project may not be completely accurate.

Therefore, you will be wanting to protect yourself financially during the project and you can do that building certain concepts and phraseology into and around the initial Scope of Work that you create. These concepts include the following:

• Build a Statement of Assumptions section into your proposal. As you address unclear aspects of work within the SOW, you will be forced to make assumptions as to what you need to do within the project to complete it to the client's satisfaction. Make every effort to remember to document every assumption you are making within your Statement of Assumptions in your proposal. If you end up in a situation where you have a documented assumption that proves to be incorrect yet the Client has signed off on your proposal with that Assumption included within it, you have protection financially for working in alignment with the original assumption made and you can point the Client back to it and sometimes save the project and maintain good Client relationships if you have this to point back to if a dispute arises.

• In a related vein, after you have won the engagement and are working with the Client to complete the Engagement Letter, you have an opportunity to work through the assumptions individually to determine their accuracy or inaccuracy prior to engagement letter finalizing and signing so both you and the Client start the project with a clearer understanding of what needs to be done. There will be less surprises and you have a chance before signing the final Engagement Letter to adjust the total price for the project and the SOW if need be.

• Try to avoid "Fixed Bid" projects. Wherever possible, try to obtain the engagement under a "Time and Materials" contract. If you need to, put a cap on the Time and Materials proposal with a statement that go something like this "Our estimated total cost for this project including contingency is $XXXXX. We will not exceed this total cost amount without your express written approval to do so." Managing project costs band client expectations through the project delivery effort then becomes the responsibility of the Consultant Project Manager, and strategies for doing a good job of this will be included within the next course in this series.

• Build in a Project Contingency. Briefly mentioned in the above point as well, in every project you do where you have to specify some form of total project cost estimate, estimate the total project costs based on expected hours, rates and expenses and build in a contingency percentage. The higher the project risk, the higher you would build your contingency amount. For example: You would need little contingency for a project to install a new operating system on a number of client desktops.  But if the client wanted you to build them a new "Social Media company that does things nobody else does today without defining it further, your contingency cost estimates would be enormous.

If you are writing a proposal after receiving an informal request for one from say a client you have worked for in the past, you may be able to just write one out and submit it because you already know a lot about the client situation and can feel safe to do so.

However, if you are informally asked to submit a proposal to a potential client whom you have not worked for in the past and where you have no in depth knowledge of them or their operations, it is always product to request at a minimum a meeting with their key stakeholders and domain knowledge experts prior to submitting your proposal so that you can learn more about them and what is needed first.

In instances where the project will prove to be a large and/or complex one, you may want to consider trying to contract the Client first to do an initial fact finding/current situation and needs assessment project first undertaken by a very knowledgeable resource from your organization – or yourself prior to writing the main proposal.

Bottom line, the more you know about the Client and what needs to be done prior to building the initial SOW for your project, the safer both you and the Client will be as there will be fewer "surprises" occurring when the project finally starts getting delivered.

# CREATING THE CLIENT ENGAGEMENT LETTER

Once you have been selected by the client verbally or by e-mail to undertake a project, it is often prudent to create an engagement letter that summaries all of the key terms of the agreement between you both. This letter is important from several perspectives including:

- A signed Letter of Engagement (LOE) allows you to contact and activate your team members (if it is a team based project you have proposed) so they can finalize their commitments to you that they are on board to work the project, start to make their travel arrangements to get to the client site, start to prepare materials, templates, etc. they will be wanting to use on the project, etc.
- A signed letter of engagement will protect you and the client and it will give you both a clear outline of what has been agreed to so there will be fewer misunderstandings that may occur once the project commences.
- All key stakeholders in the project will know what is to be delivered, when things will start, when they are expected to conclude, etc.

Key things that an Engagement Letter should contain (as and where they are important to project success) include the following:

- The start date for the project and expected completion date

- Summaries of any important project dates, milestones or key decision points during the project that may change project scope, timelines, or direction
- Responsibilities of the Client to ensure project success.
- Agreed to terms for a Decision Request process to be implemented if one is deemed necessary
- Names of all contractors to be used on the project, their start dates and their bill or chargeout rates
- Terms for all travel and expense costs to be borne by each of the signing parties
- A statement of project scope – what is to be included and what is to be excluded, usually referencing back to the original proposal suggested plans, dates, resources and scope of work to be completed.
- Terms for space, equipment and application access requirements for the team on the client site
- A high level project plan for at a minimum, the first phase of the project. Note: Sometimes a "Phase Zero" occurs where the consulting Team leader goes on site first to work all of the upcoming project logistics with the client assigned project representatives. This may occur either before or after the Engagement Letter has actually been signed.
- Documentation of key project assumptions, critical success factors and special considerations where they may be a factor in project completion.
- Space for both the Consultant and for the Client Acceptor to sign and date to finalize the agreement.

Please note that some projects will actually commence with one or two key project leaders coming to the site to further scope out activities to be completed.  This is sometimes done under a Letter of Intent (LOI) as opposed to an Engagement Letter as further research, discussion and agreement between the Consultant and the client may need to occur prior to the Engagement Letter being signed off.

A formal Letter of Engagement is not necessary for all projects.  Use of it is often determined by the Consultant as he/she/the Consulting Entity determines whether or not the complexity of the project, project risks, size and scope of the project, etc. warrants its inclusion as part of the project official commitments that need to be documented.  As mentioned, use of this letter is optional for a project and only you the Consultant can determine whether or not it needs to be completed.

However, if you do have it in place, it can at least provide both you and the Client with additional protection and a point of reference to what was agreed to at project commencement; and this sometimes helps to keep the relationships solid as issues around scope, cost, project duration, resources, etc. arise later that may need to be discussed or explained.

# CREATING THE HIGH LEVEL PROJECT PLAN

The high level project plan is the first project plan built on a project and its use and purpose is to create an overview of the steps that need to be taken to complete the project, which resources will be expected to complete each step and how much time it is expected to take them, it documents their proposed resource chargeout rates plus contingency allowances and is an integral part of documenting the proposed costs to complete the project that are submitted within the proposal. This High Level Plan is usually included as a component to both the Engagement Letter and the submitted proposal.

Naturally, all project plans created are different with respect to the steps required to complete each project but the template below should give you some idea as to what the High level Project Plan could look like in terms of structure.

| Stages | | PM/BA | Lead* | Totals |
|---|---|---|---|---|
| **Stage 0** | **Project Initiation** | | | |
| | Preparation | 2.0 | | 2.0 |
| | Project Kickoff Meeting | 0.5 | 0.5 | 1.0 |
| | Project Plan Finalization | 0.5 | 0.5 | 1.0 |
| | Project Administration Workshop | 0.2 | 0.2 | 0.4 |
| | Roles & Responsibilities Summary | 0.5 | 0.2 | 0.7 |
| | Initial Review of Client Documentation | | 1.0 | 1.0 |
| | Create Questionaires | | 2.0 | 2.0 |
| | Develop Project Memo | 0.5 | 0.2 | 0.7 |
| **Stage 1** | **Enterprise Model and Requirements** | | | |
| Step 1 | *Review Business* | | | |
| | Preparation | 0.5 | 0.5 | 1.0 |
| | Review Strategic Plans | 1.0 | 1.0 | 3.5 |
| | Review Vision Materials | 1.0 | 1.0 | |
| | Develop Memo of Understanding | 0.5 | 2.0 | 4.0 |
| | Gain Acceptance of Memo | 0.5 | 0.5 | 1.0 |
| etc. - not all project steps displayed.... | | | | |
| | Develop Implementation Strategy Report | 3.0 | 3.0 | 9.0 |
| | Develop Business Case Document | 2.0 | 2.0 | |
| | Revise and Accept Plan & Report | 2.0 | 1.0 | 4.5 |
| | Close Project | 1.0 | | 1.0 |
| Total Days | | 66.2 | 63.6 | 230.3 |
| Contingency @ 5% | | 3.3 | 3.2 | 11.5 |
| Days incl. Contingency | | 69.5 | 66.8 | 241.8 |
| 2.2 Rate/Day | | $870 | $930 | |
| 4.0 Rate/Day | | $1,590 | $1,700 | |
| Cost @ 2.2 Rate | | $60,474 | $62,105 | $ 285,051 |
| Cost @ 4.0 Rate | | $110,521 | $113,526 | $ 521,428 |
| Utilization Percentage: 70 days = 100% | | 99% | 95% | |

Within a proposal effort, the High Level Project Plan works with the Scope of Work and documented assumptions to frame up the work effort to be undertaken for the Client. Core components to the High level Project Plan include the following:

Project Stages – These should be clearly defined in a multi-stage project as there will often be deliverable by stage to be promised to the Client, often involving key decisions to be made by the Client as the project moves forward.

An Overview of Project Tasks within each stage and the Deliverables at key points in the process are documented

Total Estimated Days by Resource by Task are shown

Contingency Rates are calculated

Note: the 2.2 Rate/Day is Internal – Client Sees Only the Retail 4.0 Rate in His/Her Version – Use whatever wholesale rate that works for your own internal purposes here. This is often used to help you keep track of your margins and expected net profits to be made on the project.

Total project utilizations by resource are shown

Total Days and Costs are calculated – by Person and for the Whole Project

These are the core components that comprise a high level project plan and they should tie-in and directly reflect the information provided in the Scope of Work.

This is a component to the proposal that you will almost always be discussing in detail with the Client prior to final Engagement Letter completion and signoff so it is a very good idea to take your time and be as accurate as you can when completing this.

If you are doing calculations and making notes in background as you complete this, keep them in a legible enough format so that if you do end up discussing the plan with the Client in your final negotiations, you can refer to your notes and even show them to your Client when he/she asks how you came up with your time and task estimates. You will be glad you did.

## ENSURING YOUR PROJECT COSTS ARE COVERED AND THAT YOU GET PAID

As a consultant, you have very little to no protection by Government agencies should a client choose to not pay you for services rendered. You are afforded no such rights by Government Agency that an employee receives so you have to be careful in your financial dealings with Clients.

As such, it will be incumbent on you to either go after the client yourself through a legal action to get money owed, or to find a way to reconcile your issues with the Client withholding payment, seek a settlement with the Client if you can to at least get partial payment for your services, or to walk away and eat the loss.

So how do you avoid this situation as a consultant or at least minimize the amounts you might lose or the frequencies that this occurs to you? Here are some tips that will help you.

• Build a strong SOW and List of Assumptions beforehand as part of your proposal and Engagement Letter. The more you have backing you up in documentation, the more you are able to hold discussions and negotiations with the Client to try to come to a settlement if a disagreement occurs.
• Try to get a retainer for travel expenses incurred to get to the project site and city at the beginning of the project. You can then setup an arrangement for repayment of this amount when your first bill is submitted. In this manner, you can at least protect your out of pocket expenses on a project which will

make life easier – then your just risking billable time as opposed to real out of pocket money.

• As changes to direction, scope, resources, etc. occur during the course of a project, be sure to document each change of anything in periodic project reports to be signed off by both parties and also diligently use both Change Requests and Decision Requests throughout your project, pushing for signoffs as the project unfolds. Again, the more you document and get written signoffs on, the more you can protect yourself financially.

• Never lose e-mails you have sent the Client or received from a Client. Find a way to keep them and store them elsewhere outside of a Client's servers. These may be useful to you if a litigation starts to occur between you.

• Never let a problem get big. If you have a chance to sort it out when it is still a small problem with the Client, it will save you potential grief.

• Build regular status reports that are delivered to the Client that document that period's achievements of the Team. Get signoffs and keep copies of these off-site as you go.

• Get weekly time sheets from your team, again, get signoffs from the client on each weekly time sheet submitted as you can.

• Be sure to incorporate in your project documentation with the Client what constitutes a "Breach" in the agreement between you and what the consequences will be if a breach occurs. Then, act as necessary to protect yourself – see the next point in this regard.

- If a Client starts to miss payment deadlines, i.e., he begins to start slow paying you and the lags in payment start to get over-long, if you have warned him or can't get him to explain to your satisfaction why the payments are so slow; if you feel any uncertainty about getting paid, pull your team until payment is made. If you have work done but not yet delivered, keep it off-site as additional leverage.
- Take good notes at all Client interfacing meetings. Particularly management level ones where project issues are being discussed. You can always point back to these if you have to and they can be used as evidence in a court action.

At the end of all of this, if you are managing your project carefully, your exposure will be less and if everything completed for the client is regularly documented and signed off, your chance of winning a litigation is improved if it comes to that. You cannot fully protect yourself from a Client unwilling to pay, but you can minimize both the risks and the damage done through following the tips listed above.

# THE CONFIDENTIALITY / NON-DISCLOSURE AGREEMENT

The Confidentiality Agreement or Non-Disclosure Agreement is often used between a client and a consultant prior to an engagement being undertaken, although there are times when it is used after an engagement has commenced. Often, in order to write a proposal that truly addresses the work that a client needs completed, a client will request that an "NDA" be signed before disclosure of client proprietary information is made available to the consultant.

Reciprocally, the consultant may request that an NDA be signed prior to a proposal being written in order to protect his/her own proprietary information such as methodologies, tools to be used on the engagement, etc.

Consultants should keep a template of one of these in their toolkits so they can bring the out to use as needed with a client – shows professionalism

If you don't know how to read and understand one of these, I recommend you have a session with a lawyer so that you can gain a full understanding before using one as part of a project or a project bid process

Following are the key components of an NDA or Confidentiality Agreement:

• Who is party to the terms of the NDA – i.e., what participants do the terms of the document apply to.

- Definition of what is and is not covered by the NDA (knowhow, products, trade secrets, etc.)
- Terms of Agreement for the NDA
- NDA term (who long is the NDA to remain in force)
- What can and cannot be copied
- What must be returned to the other party on term completion and by whom
- What constitutes a breach of the agreement
- What penalties are required to be paid by the offending party if a breach occurs
- Terms under which the agreement may be terminated prior to full term of the agreement being reached

The agreement must then be Signed and dated by all participating parties.

As a consultant, you will be viewing consulting opportunities on bulleting boards and occasionally, head hunters will be contacting you with opportunities to work on projects. They will often be making reference as to whether or not the opportunity is a W2 or a 1099 project or is open to both types of employment.

So here is the difference between the two employment methods.

### W2 Employment Contract - USA

A W2 contract or employment agreement means in effect that you are to be working on salary. This may still be a term contract and you may have been placed on site by a consulting company you have affiliations with but in the client's eyes you are in effect an employee and employee deductions and benefits normally in place with other standard employees of that company will apply to you as well. These could include such things as:

- Social security, Medicare, and income tax are withheld
- The company pays 1/2 of social security and Medicare and must carry workmen's compensation coverage
- Your earnings count towards eligibility for future unemployment compensation
- If you do not get paid, the government may be able to assist for free
- You are protected by FMLA, COBRA, etc., laws.

Any deals you might have with the head hunting or consulting group you are affiliated with would be out of sight of the client company you would be working for under the contract you create with them.

Canadians filling out the right paperwork are able to work under W2 contracts in the USA (I.E. – They can get H1 or "TN" status to work in the USA. But while working there under this status, they will be contributing to the US government as an employee would and they would still be required to renew their H1 annually and travel back to Canada at least once every six months.

## 1099 Employment Contract

A 1099 contract on the other hand is what a consultant would normally be under the terms of when taking contract assignments with a client. Generally, a person who contracts to provide a service for a company as an independent contractor would usually provide their own resources, computer, tools, etc. to deliver the contracted for project although often a client needing something done using a specific piece on non-standard software would provide access to the consultant to that software for the duration of the project. 1099 consultants are usually not supervised as an employee would be by the client.

This person's earnings are usually paid out to them after receiving an invoice from them operating as an independent contractor and the IRS reporting is usually done on a Form 1099 MISC. Nothing is withheld from the Gross earnings to be paid to the consultant for SS, FICA, Etc. The consultant is responsible for calculating his or her own government taxes on revenues earned.

By the way, if the client refuses to pay you for work done, you have no protection.  This would be considered a breach of contract situation and your only recourse would be to sue the client.

## ENROLLING IN AND USING BULLETIN BOARDS

Probably one of the first places a consultant goes when looking for a new project is to an industry bulletin board that posts projects and resources needed for projects. It is also always a very good idea for a consultant to register on these sites and to keep his or her resume and skills information current on those sites along with their availability for work.

When you are looking, also make a point of adding something to your profile, resume, etc. on these sites so that something "fresh" has been posted for you. This often will help you to be served up first as potential resourcers for projects and clients are searching. A newer date stamp on a changed profile record is often all it takes for you to be highlighted as a currently available resource.

### Major USA Consultant Resourcing Bulletin Boards

Among consultants, probably the most well-known and widely used resourcing bulletin board is called "Dice" and can be found at http://www.dice.com. Dice has been around for many, many years and I have landed several projects from it in my past. Just by being registered on it with an available resume and skills matrix posted to it, gets me regular e-mails from various resourcers looking to staff projects.

What types of consultants should be posting on Dice? Just about anyone in a professional business or technology consulting profession should be there. Its primary focus is to finding technology skills based projects for contractors, but there are many financial services, human resources, marketing and other consulting discipline related opportunities that can be found there as well.

Dice works both ways. Resourcers can find you and contact you and you can search for projects and resources needed and directly contact the resourcers who have posted a need for a resource through this system as well.

http://searchnow.com – This is a good place for consultants to find projects requiring resources. Search Now operates in both Canada and the USA

## Regional USA Consultant Resourcing Bulletin Boards

Regional bulletin boards usable by consultants in the USA often include:

http://www.pyramidci.com - A good organization to get registered with as a professional management and IT consultant is Pyramid Consulting, Inc. out of Alpharetta, Georgia. I registered with them years ago and still regularly get invitations from them to participate on engagements all across the USA.

## Major Canadian Consultant Resourcing Bulletin Boards

http://www.simplyhired.ca – is a great Canadian job and contract posting bulletin board. Put your desired type of project or job into the system, give them your e-mail address and location, and you will receive daily opportunities in your e-mail box for you to consider applying for.

http://eagleonline.com/ - Also know as the "Eagle's Nest is an excellent Canadian project and job staffing agency. Get registered into their database and you will receive job and project newsletters and opportunities for projects matching your skillset that you can apply for.

http://ca.indeed.com – A bulletin board for consulting opportunities Canada wide.

http://ca.searchnow.com – A good place for consultants to find projects requiring resources. Search Now operates in both Canada and the USA

TEKsystems, Inc. – https://www.teksystems.com/ - A solid Canada based I.T. resources recruiter. It annually deploys over 70,000 resources on projects throughout North America, Europe and Asia.

## Local and Regional Canadian Consultant Resourcing Bulletin Boards

If you are wanting to find a project in a certain geography, do not neglect the local and regional staffing organizations. For example, a couple of organizations in B.C., Canada that will retain your resume and will look to get you in on projects as they come available and they are preparing bids for include as examples

Annex Consulting Group – http://www.annexgroup.com – mostly a provider of IT and Business consulting opportunities based out of Vancouver.

Ignite Technical Resources – http://ignitechnical.com
– IT contractor resourcing for the Vancouver and lower
mainland of B.C. area

By the way, don't neglect public bulletin boards such as
"Craig's List" or "Kijiji". Sometimes you can get paying
projects or small engagements out of these types of
sites as well, particularly for doing things like building
websites, writing articles, freelance e-books, etc.

**Public Service Bulletin Boards**

Another type of bulletin board and notification type of
site for projects include the provincial and federal
project bulletin boards in Canada – each province has
one and there is a federal one out there as well. And
there are similar state and federal ones available in the
USA also. A quick search through your browser can
help you find ones that you might be interested in
registering through. Also, there are international ones
out there you can find through online searches that will
give you an opportunity to register on as well.

It's just a matter of doing a little research online to find
these sites and then following their guidelines to get
registered for the types of projects you might wish to
complete. Note – also be searching for "tenders" and
"bid tenders" – more for industrial types of projects
but you can occasionally find projects through these
types of bulletin boards as well – particularly for
projects like supplying technologies, computers,
technology maintenance contracts, office equipment
maintenance, etc.

One important thing to keep in mind. If you start
looking to contract in the public sector, you will usually

be competing against all the larger consulting firms who all get notified on every competitive bid project that comes out and they are usually the ones landing these types of projects. Often, your best strategy to get into one of these types of projects is to signup to get these same notifications and then if you see something that is a fit for your skills, partner with one of the larger consulting organizations to get into the project.

If you are a very strong fit, you can also offer to them your willingness to draft the initial proposal response or Statement of Work for the project – they like that – it saves them tedious work and the project gets to ultimately go out under their name anyway. The other strategy of competing against the entities with your own team is tougher – but if you have a group with the right skills and you aren't afraid of doing the heavy work of proposal writing, you can give it a go yourself.

My end thought on this – having done much of this sort of work myself, is that this is something you evolve to in your career. Before even attempting something like this, you should have some very significant template toolkits in your own consulting toolkit because this is a lot of work. The easiest ways for you to get into public sector work is to go through a larger firm as a sub-contracted resource or focus on the private sector bulletin boards such as "Dice" to get yourself working as an independent.

Time though will increase your contacts, your consulting toolkit and your ability to go after more sophisticated projects that require teams to complete.

Published articles will bring your business credibility a long way. I have published a number of articles on the Internet and it has brought me inquiries about my services and traffic to my websites. For example, I like to publish articles I think to write on http://ezinearticles.com who distributes globally. Now when I search for my name on Google, I find my articles with my name attached looking back at me from literally dozens of different websites so this does work to help build your name in the public domain.

Below are two business articles I have written to give you a couple of examples as to the kinds of things you can write and publish to help enhance your credibility in your own profession. FYI – they like to see you publish articles in the 800-1200 word range – these distribute the best.

## Technology has Changed the Fabric of Successful Corporations

Over the course of my consulting career, I have found many similarities in the problems facing many corporations. One reason why there is a "repetitive theme" to the types of problems I encounter is that many large organizations I consult to still are very "hierarchical" in structure. This is a popular form of organizational structure that has been prevalent for many decades and has been particularly effective in manufacturing organizations. A key reason for the wide use of this sort of structure was that, for many years, information systems had difficulty in supporting more flexible organizational structures.

Today however, relational systems, client /server technologies, virtual computing environments, Cloud Computing, and the Internet explosion as a whole has made it easier to share information across geographically distributed organizations; to market the organization globally in concert with social media platforms and 3rd party interfacing, new object-oriented development approaches have improved the flexibility of applications to better meet the needs of more end users and customers; and data warehousing/data mining, imaging, EDI and workflow technologies have made it easier to dramatically improve internal business processes, provide better business modeling and forecasting capabilities, and reduce operating costs.

In the past dozen years or so, a paradigm shift has taken place in the way people think about corporations. Project and process teams are replacing divisions; decisions are being made at all levels of a corporation as opposed to management only; management structures are flattening with managers becoming more like hands-on coaches working alongside other team members rather than monitoring and controlling from the top; and workgroup/account manager structures are replacing segmented 'task' based structures where each employee is asked to do only a few components of the process before handing units of work off to be completed by others in the chain. Benefits organization are reaping through this type of restructuring are enormous and are eliminating a large number of inefficiencies that are inherent to hierarchically structured organizations including:

- Customer service is improving dramatically - no longer are customers shunted from department to department to get answers, now they are able to establish relationships with individual 'account managers' who can answer all their questions, make decisions on their behalf, and provide them with all the support and comfort they desire.
- Decisions can be made much more quickly, usually within the process teams as each team is represented by personnel from different parts of the process cycle. This type of fluid structure can greatly reduce new product and service development times, as approvals no longer have to go through multiple channels in a number of departments.
- The quality of products and services increase as people are no longer being asked to make decisions or approve product designs/service offerings with only very focused frames of reference. Through daily exposure to other team members, they can now make decisions based on a much broader understanding of the issues making their own individual expertise much more useful.
- No longer are divisional performance objectives obtained at the expense of the total enterprise. Managers are no longer more concerned about achieving results in their own departments than they are in achieving corporate profitability and service targets.
- Empowered employees are now much more useful to the corporation. As they are now being asked

to contribute their knowledge to project teams instead of being asked to perform only simple tasks, the corporation know has a much broader knowledge base upon which to improve corporate effectiveness.

• Facilities costs and direct internal marketing expenses are reducing as more and more corporations are enabling staff to work from home. Many organizations now also contract out many of their services to stay at home entrepreneurs – such as "social media" marketing of their products, independent testing and reviews of their products, making use of $3^{rd}$ party "sales channels" to build advertising and distribute it, etc.

The above are just a few of the benefits that corporations who have gone through the pain of transformation have experienced. Organizations including Sony, Google, Ford, WalMart, IBM, Dell and General Motors to name just a few have all undertaken these transformations and have greatly improved their competitiveness and profitability as a result.

To conclude, it is evident that organizations need to build ongoing process re-engineering into the fabric of their organizations and that Marketing and IT departmentally and knowledge-wise need to become equal partners in the vision and direction setting activities that a corporation undertakes. Corporations ignore the power of social media, the Internet and today's rapid technological innovation in the marketplace in general at their peril as today, these are not just strategic competitive weapons; they are corporate survival itself – and corporations need to constantly adapt or get left behind.

## Corporate Message Management Risk Avoidance

Beyond the capabilities that corporations need to have in their messaging platforms from a business usefulness perspective, they need to be thinking about implementing capabilities in their messaging infrastructures that ensure that the e-mails they send out get into the hands of the people they are sending them out to.

In addition to the importance of efficiently sending out millions of messages daily where messages need to go out quickly, without fail and they have to "Reach" recipients, outbound IP addresses have to be White Listed as far as is possible with every ISP globally. This means not just passively sending messages in the hopes that they get there, it means:

• Taking pro-active steps to get "White Listed", monitoring ISP's continually to ensure that the corporation remains white listed, and knowing how and when to act when issues start to occur within an ISP so that it can pro-actively sort out an issue before becoming "Black Listed".
• Monitoring where ISP's put e-mails that are sent out. For example, are they getting sent to a user's primary e-mail address, do they get blocked or does the ISP send the corporation's messages to junk mail? A corporation's messaging platform also should then have the capability to correct the blocking and Junk mail scenarios with these ISP's when they occur.
• Keeping a corporation's used "IP Addresses" clean, usable and recognizable globally as being OK to deliver and OK to receive by each mail service ISP.
• Monitor ISP's to ensure each e-mail sent to them gets delivered to an authentic account holder and

if an e-mail address sent out is invalid, the corporation needs an internal system that instantly blocks us from sending out a second e-mail to a "dead-drop" to avoid being blocked by an ISP for sending messages to dead e-mail accounts.

Additional individual message management and control capabilities that should be implemented also include:

• Ensuring message header verbiage and content pass scrutiny by ISP's reading them for certain "Key Words" that could label them as potential spam
• Ensuring that every e-mail sent out has an opt-out feature available to the recipient and ensuring that the corporation does not send a second e-mail after an opt-out to avoid SPAM complaints which also can get the corporation black listed.
• Depending on the corporation's volume considerations, it may need to have a "Revolving Set" of virtual, valid IP addresses that are used to send out messages to always try to reduce the volume of e-mails sent to individual ISP's as they will block high volumes of e-mails coming in from one IP address.
• The corporation will need to in an automated fashion, "cleanse e-mail send out lists against suppressed and banned email addresses
• Automate the subscriber grievance response process to ensure each grievance is addressed quickly and consistently to a customer's satisfaction.
• Automatically manage bounces in a professional way as they occur to avoid getting blocked or "Black Listed" by an ISP.

In looking for your solution, remember also that higher-end solutions that are able to solve all or most of the above considerations are usually implemented on your internal servers as this gives you the most control of your messaging systems and IP addressing solutions. This is an added implementation cost that you will need to factor into your solution. Remember that you will need to build in certain levels of fault tolerance in your solution – this means server redundancy, automatic fail-over features in case of a crash, and automated IP address fail-over solutions in case an IP address you are using gets compromised.

If you opt for a lesser solution, you will probably be looking at some form of service bureau implementation and they will have their own concerns about the safety of their shared IP addresses that you would be using on their platforms. And it is not unheard of to have some other organization who shares your outbound physical IP address to bring you down occasionally if their message management processes are not strong enough from a risk avoidance perspective. So be prepared with a fail-over plan if you must use one of these solutions for your enterprise.

The purchase decision for the message management platform you ultimately select and implement for your corporation will naturally be predicated on the volume and types of messages you need to send out, the importance on these messages getting into the hands of the people you send the messages to, and the criticality of your enterprise that the messages get sent out and accepted. For example, what will it cost you if you are "black-listed" with ISP's for a week or two and you can't get your messages out to your intended recipients?

Putting in "fail-safe" or close to fail-safe solutions for your message management platforms will cost you more money to implement but be fully aware of what it could cost you if your messaging systems fail you for any length of time.

# CREATING AN MP4 VIDEO PRESENTATION USING MICROSOFT POWERPOINT

Recently, I had been wanting to build better view-ability into my lecture videos and so I had begun experimenting with Microsoft PowerPoint to see how I could use their slide animation and slide transition features and then possibly capture this using a screen capture and recording tool to make my presentations more appealing.

As I worked with PowerPoint itself, I learned some things about adding animations and audio and then using PowerPoint itself to record and build my MP4 videos in such a manner that a screen capture tool was not needed at all. The entire process from start to finish could be done from within the PowerPoint environment except for the creation of the audio.

This is how you do it.

**Step 1:** Open up PowerPoint and select the template you wish to use for your presentation – or create a custom one.

**Step 2:** Build your base presentation.

**Step 3:** Structure Your Animations – i.e., how do you want your bullets and images to appear, fade away, etc. within each slide. To work with slide animations, click on the "Animations" tab on the screen you wish to work on. Click on a block of text, bullet points, image you want to work on, etc. and the Animations bar will highlight at the top of the screen to allow you to start to set your animation options. Note: You can also click on the "Animation Pane" to the right to open up a side window allowing you additional "advanced" capabilities to work with your animations. Double clicking on an item in your Animation Pane by the way, will bring up a window with even more animation settings that you can work with. Experiment until you have everything working the way you want.

Tip: If you want to use the same animation techniques for a series of slides, then once you have completed the first slide to your satisfaction, make copies of this slide elsewhere in your presentation after first saving it and the animation settings will travel with every additional copy made.

**Step4:** Script the audio you wish to create and then record and edit it using your standard audio recording and editing toolset.

**Step 5:** Import the audio to your lecture. To do this, go to your first slide and under the "Insert" tab, select "Insert Audio" in the "Media" section of the header options. Find your recorded and edited audio on your computer and import it. A speaker and audio play bar will appear on your slide. Position this on your slide where you would have it show as on your first slide when done, the speaker will still appear in your final production.

**Step 6**: Set up your audio so that it will run across all your slides in background. To do this, highlight the speaker that has appeared on your first slide by clicking on it and then click on the "Design" header tab. Under the "Audio Tools" tab that appears, select "Playback" when the next options appear underneath, first select "Play in Background". To the left, select the options to "Start Automatically", "Play Across Slides" and "Hide During Show".

**Step 7:** Save what you have created thus far.

**Step 8:** Go to Slide Show and press the "Record Slide Show" button. When the window appears, select the option for "slide and animation timings" then press the "Start Recording" button. As the presentation starts to record, you should be hearing the audio and the screen animations and slide transitions will occur each time you click a mouse. Click your way through the entire presentations, synchronizing the animations and transitions with the audio as you go until you reach the end of the audio and presentation. Save your work.

**Step 9:** Click the "File" tab then click the "Export" tab. On the next screen, click the "Create a Video" button. Click the "Use Recorded Timings and Narrations" button then when the drop list opens below, click the next "Use Recorded Timings and Narrations" option that appears then click the "Create Video" button.

**Step 10:** Define your recording name and where you want the recording to be stored on your computer, press "Save" and your recording will start to process. Give the process time to complete – could take some time if it is a long presentation.

Upon completion, you now have an animated PowerPoint presentation built into an MP4 video that you can use standalone or even add as a component into a more sophisticated lecture you may be creating using your standard video recording and editing tools. It will view just like a PowerPoint slideshow you would have created for an office lecture or presentation – but now you can upload it to the Internet in full video MP4 format.

So where you wish to present PowerPoint lectures to the masses, this could be a good approach for you to use.

# THE ACUITY TIME BOOKING AND SCHEDULING SYSTEM

If your new home business will involve you providing services for others where they would be booking for and paying for your time, then you may want to consider making a small investment and obtain the Acuity System for your website or Blog site.

The Acuity Scheduling System allows you to:

- Set your terms for various types of projects you might wish to undertake for others
- To have your purchasers then schedule your available time to assist them
- They can view your calendar to see your available times (you can block out your calendar for time you want to keep for yourself)
- It ties in directly to PayPal (credit card purchases accepted as well) where you can define how they pay you. Up front, portion up front, on completion, etc.
- These purchase records and histories of work you have done for people are exportable to accounting packages or are downloadable.
- Your clients can even setup login accounts of their own with you.

This is a professional level product - and I looked at over 20 or so before selecting and now recommending this one which I use on my site and have implemented elsewhere as well. Following are some more details on this product suite.

## Acuity Scheduling System Overview

The Acuity Time Booking and Scheduling System is not just a system I have come across and have chosen to represent. This is actually a system that I use on my Howtoguru.club website and it is a system that I have also implemented for a client of mine who runs a Home Nursing Business.

We have both been using this system for some time and have been very pleased with it – so what you will be getting here is a five star in favor rating on this product from a happy user of the product. It does all the things we both needed it to do for our respective businesses and we have found it to be an extremely flexible product to configure for our businesses feature-wise yet very intuitive during setup, configuration, and putting it into production on our sites.

### What the Product Does

The Acuity Time Booking and Scheduling System is built to give your business a method of being able to have people book/schedule your company's services or the time of one or more people in your company online from your website. You can set it up for people who come to your website to schedule their own appointments and even have them pay you up front as part of the process (at your option) before they are allowed to schedule the time.

If you are constantly on the move, you can get this system to send an e-mail/text to your phone to notify you whenever someone has made a booking so you can even manage this system while on the run.

## *"I don't have to have awkward conversations requesting to get paid."*

### Features of the system

This system has numerous setup / configuration options providing you with many features including the following:

- Setup various appointment types and rates for services
- Integrate appointment setup with PayPal to collect payments (optional)
- Block out times when you are unavailable – customers can only book during times you want them to
- Get notified on your phone and/or by e-mail whenever an appointment is made
- Set up forms on signup so you can get up front the information you need from your client to manage all aspects of the booking
- Clients can setup recurring bookings
- Comes with an online viewable calendar showing when booking times are available

- You can easily print off your daily schedule so you know what you need to do and where you need to go
- Automatically have clients fill out forms or agreements
- Setup courses, events, seminars, etc.
- Include a Map and location information for your clients
- Mobile application for iPhone, iPad and Android
- Multi-currency system
- Integrates with over 200 3$^{rd}$ party applications and websites including: Facebook, Google Calendar, Go to Meeting, Outlook, Quick Books, Mail Chimp, AWeber, Constant Contact, WordPress, Squarespace and more...
- Clients can setup accounts with you and can track their booking histories
- Customize the system with your own Brand, logos, etc.
- Affiliate program is available

## CONFIDENTIALITY AND NON-DISCLOSURE
## AGREEMENT

This agreement is made and entered into this
_____ 2005, between
Example, Inc. ("Example") and
_____
("Company") a _____ whose principal
address is at
_____
_____. As used herein, the terms
"Example" and "Company" shall include each of their
respective employees and agents.

WHEREAS, each party hereto will be providing
the other with certain information of a confidential or a
proprietary nature; and

WHEREAS, in order for each party to provide
such information, the parties require certain
assurances and promises by the other related to the
confidentiality of the Disclosing Party's (as defined
below) data, records or other information presented to
or to which the receiving party has access.

NOW THEREFORE, for and in exchange of
valuable consideration, the receipt that is hereby
acknowledged, the parties agree as follows:

"Confidential and Proprietary Information" means all
information furnished by either Example or Company

as the owner of and disclosure of such of its confidential and proprietary information, ("Disclosing Party"), in connection with the Proposal, including, without limiting the generality of the foregoing; trade secrets, customer lists or data, business records and documents, marketing studies, profits, costs, pricing, program results, business plans and records, and all other materials, whether written or oral, tangible or intangible with respect to the Proposal, which such party holds confidential and has not publicly disclosed.

Each party agrees as follows:

To maintain the confidentiality of the Disclosing Party's Confidential and Proprietary Information including but not limited to providing the same degree of care to avoid disclosure or unauthorized use of the Confidential and Proprietary Information as the receiving party provides to its own Confidential and Proprietary Information, and to retain the Confidential and Proprietary Information in a secure place with access limited to senior management of the receiving party evaluating the Proposal.

To direct its employees and agents to maintain the strictest confidentiality and present the Disclosing Party's Confidential and Proprietary Information to only those employees and authorized representatives with an absolute need to know in connection with the Proposal;

To not disclose Confidential and Proprietary Information to any third party (other than advisors who shall be directed to maintain the confidentiality), including but not limited to subcontractors, without written authorization form the Disclosing Party.

To use the Disclosing Party's Confidential and Proprietary Information solely in connection with its evaluation of the Proposal;

To indemnify and hold harmless the Disclosing Party from any and all loss, damage or liability which may result from unauthorized disclosure by the receiving party of the Confidential and Proprietary Information; and

That all work produced in connection with, or related to, each Disclosing Party's Confidential and Proprietary Information shall be the sole property of the Disclosing Party.

To immediately notify the Disclosing Party of any information which comes to its attention, which does or might indicate there has been any loss of confidentiality of such Disclosing Party's Confidential and Proprietary Information.

1.	Within thirty (30) days following written notice by the Disclosing Party, the receiving party shall return to the Disclosing Party all materials, including all copies received or created in connection with this Agreement.  No copies shall be made or retained by the receiving party.  All Confidential and Proprietary Information of the Disclosing Party remains the property of the Disclosing Party.

2.	Example and Company agree that should this Agreement be breached; money damages alone would be inadequate compensation.  Accordingly, in addition to any other remedies available at law or in equity, any court of competent jurisdiction may also enjoin the disclosure or use by the receiving party of any confidential and Proprietary Information of the

Disclosing Party. The laws of the State of Texas shall govern this agreement. This Agreement may be amended only by, and waiver of any term must be in, a writing executed by authorized representatives of Example and Company.

3.    No agency or partnership relationship is created by this Agreement. No rights, obligations, representations or terms other than those expressly set forth herein are to be implied from this Agreement. In particular, without limitation, no license is hereby granted directly or indirectly by either party.

4.    A receiving party of Confidential and Proprietary Information shall have no obligation with respect to information which a) on the date hereof is generally known to the public, b) subsequent to disclosure hereunder is lawfully received from a third party having rights therein without restriction of dissemination, c) prior to disclosure hereunder was within the legitimate possession of the receiving party and which can be confirmed by contemporaneous written documentation, d) the release of which is authorized previously in writing by the Disclosing Party, or e) is ordered to be produced by a court of competent jurisdiction.

The obligations set forth herein shall survive for a period of one (1) year from the date hereof.

This Agreement shall survive the execution of any subsequent agreements related to the subject matter hereof, or the failure of either party to execute any substantive agreement regarding the Proposal. Any termination of this Agreement shall not relieve either party of any of its then outstanding and unfulfilled obligations under this Agreement or from any obligation that arises upon termination or is intended to survive termination.

| Example, Inc. | | Company | |
|---|---|---|---|
| By: | | By: | |
| Title: | | Title: | |
| Date: | | Date: | |

This attachment provides the reader with a template
for a Client Engagement Letter.

- Confidential Report – Template Consulting

# Letter of Engagement

## Submitted

## For Client, Inc.

### Submitted August 3, 2016

## Important Confidentiality Notice

# Engagement Overview

This letter is a companion to the "Initial Proposal" recently completed for Client by Template personnel. The initial proposal contains the details of the project to be completed for which this Letter of Engagement is being written – please refer to that document to view the full scope of services and deliverables to be completed on signed acceptance of this engagement letter.

This letter documents the terms of engagement for this phase of the project and includes the following:

- Overall Project Assumptions and Requirements
- Overview of Project Schedule
- Project Resourcing and Related Pricing
- Project Billing and Payment Terms
- Project Agreement and Signoff

# Overall Project Assumptions

Where project realities vary from the assumptions listed below, total estimated project costs and project duration estimates/completion estimates may be affected. Following are a number of project assumptions for this project:

Template Resources will be using ERwin on the project to develop the logical and physical data models required and also will be using this tool to generate the physically deployed databases that will be created during the project. In our initial report we recommended that Client purchase and use this tool for its internal staff as well. Should Client not do so, this can increase the amount of work required to complete the project and the amount of work Client will have to undertake to maintain the environment once the project consultants complete their work and leave.

Our original proposal described a project team comprised primarily of Client provided resources for all project roles. It is now our understanding that Client will be internally providing all business analyst and developer resources for the project. If Client personnel cannot be fully committed 100% to this project as and when required by the Project Plan to be constructed, then:

• The estimated project duration/completion date could be affected as work is not completed as and when needed.
• Template Consulting may have to find and insert additional consulting resources which could affect both project billed costs to Client and possibly also project completion date.
• The project will be undertaken primarily at Client' location and adequate work space including computers will be provided to Template Consulting provided resources. No travel is expected for consultants. If any travel is required to complete certain project tasks, Client will cover these additional costs incurred by Template Consulting provided resources.
• Dan Template will take on the role of both Project Manager and that of Project Lead Architect. We assume that Client will designate an internal resource to work with Dan in a Client Acceptor capacity. This person (or Client may wish to designate a second resource for this) will also take on the task of arranging space for required meetings and group work

sessions, handling any project related logistical requirements that arise, and will also ensure that the right internal staff are made available and participate in overall team workshops as required.

- We assume this project will include the development of a complete user interface (Web) environment for both customer end users. Client will inform us at project commencement which first corporate customer they wish us to build this environment for.
- This project will conclude when Release Version 1 of the system is put into the Client production environment and when internal User Acceptance Testing has been satisfactorily completed.

## Overview of Project Schedule

"Project Schedule A" in the initial proposal contains our initial estimate for the elapsed time required to complete this project. A more detailed project and resourcing plan will be completed during the first few weeks of the project. This will be a working tool within the project and will be visited and revised as required throughout the course of this effort. Microsoft Project will be used to manage this project.

Our initial project plan had an estimated start date of June 25th, 2016 with a completed and into production date estimate of approximately the end of October, 2016 or early November. As this project is commencing at the later date of August 13th, we would now estimate project completion at approximately the end of January, 2017.

Please note that if agreed to, Dan Template is willing to initiate this project during the week of August 6th to

10<sup>th</sup> working from home initially. He will begin to build the detailed Project Plan and will start to frame up some of the project deliverables and project tools/templates to be used on the project. A signature for acceptance of this earlier start date and tasks is included in the Project Agreement and Signoff Section at the end of this document.

As done previously, we have included a 20% contingency cost on this project to cover unknowns. For example:

- Dan or one of the other project resources may be pulled by Client from the project to support sales efforts or other things going on at Client from time to time – which may have time to delivery implications.
- If Client chooses not to use ERwin on the project as we recommend, the project will be harder and more time consuming to deliver.
- Client may not have all that is required for a proper development environment in place at this time – getting this all defined, and the products purchased and implemented may impact time to delivery.
- There may be times throughout the project where additional Template Consulting personnel may be utilized for short periods of time as they may have certain insights, knowledge or skills needed to complete certain project tasks or to bring in useful knowledge to aid in good decision making.
- Other unforeseen events may occur that could affect scope and time to delivery.

## Project Resourcing and Related Pricing

At this time, Template Consulting will be providing Client with two accepted resources – Dan Template and Joe Template. Both of these resources will be on site on August 15<sup>th</sup> if signoff on this engagement letter occurs by August 4<sup>th</sup>. The on-site start date will probably slip one day for each day later than this that the project signoff takes to complete.

Day rates (based on an 8-hour day) for each consultant are as follows:

• For Dan Template - $1,800 per day – landed day rate – assumes Dan is resident in your city at his cost.
• For Joe Template - $1,400 per day – landed day rate – assumes Joe is resident in your city at his cost.

See the initial project report for more detailed breakdowns of these time estimates for completion of this project. Note that if less time is required to complete this project, Template Consulting will bill Client correspondingly less.

## Project Billing and Payment Terms

Template Consulting will bill Client bi-monthly for services – covering services to the 15<sup>th</sup> and to month end respectively. Payment terms are net 15 days. As both Dan Template and Joe Template will be coming in from out of province and will be needing to pay for accommodations and travel during the first month prior to receiving their first services payments, a project advance of $5,000.00 for each consultant is requested to be paid on date of project commencement, August 15<sup>th</sup>, 2016. This project advance can be deducted from the first project billing which will be set for August 31$^{st}$, 2012.

## Project Agreement and Signoff

Below in two parts are your signoffs to commence this project, signifying agreement to the terms documented above and to the project scope defined in the originally project report completed for you this past June. Signature line one denotes your agreement for Dan Template to commence work on this project during the week of August 6$^{th}$ to 10$^{th}$ to complete as much preplanning work as he can prior to his arrival on your site on August 15$^{th}$. The second signature line confirms your agreement to the overall project. Please sign where indicated and fax the signature page back to us at your earliest convenience.

# Project Signature Page

Part 1:  Client agrees to allow Dan Template to initiate work on this project during the week of August 6th to 10th.

As per Client Inc.

_____ Date: _____

As per Template Consulting

_____ Date: _____

Dan Template – Principal

Part 2:  Client agrees to the scope and terms of this project as defined in this engagement letter and the "Initial Proposal" delivered to Client in June 2016. Template Consulting resources will commence this project onsite on August 15th, 2016.

As per Client Inc.

_____ Date: _____

As per Template Consulting

_____ Date: _____

Dan Template – Principal

Client:  Please sign, date and fax this signature page back to Template Consulting at xxx-xxx-xxxx to complete this project acceptance and initiate this project. Thankyou.

# APPENDIX – GOOD SITE LINKS TO KNOW

Please note that if the link does not take you to the site automatically, you can try to then either copy and paste it into your browser's URL line or just type it into the browser's URL line and it should get you there.

https://acuityscheduling.com:  By far the best website embeddable "time booking calendar" I have seen out there.  I use it on my own site.  It is easy to set yourself up as an affiliate seller if you are interested as well. It earns me a few dollars from time to time.

https://AdWords.google.com/KeywordPlanner#start : Google AdWords "Keyword Planner" site. You may need to setup an account with them to use this tool but it is a great resource when you are wanting to setup keyword searches for your published content and web pages.

http://allwebcodesign.com/ : A good site to get a template starter website "template" for your business. They have many to choose from and in addition, have numerous "widgets" for your site you can also purchase such as music players, video players, RSS scroll feeders, etc.

https://kdp.amazon.ca : Kindle Books self-publishing site for Canada.  Here is where you publish your new Kindle books and view reports on your sales made.

https://authorcentral.amazon.com/ : To setup an Author Page at Amazon. You can only do this after you have published a book on Kindle.

https://buffer.com:  A good site to use to schedule and publish your posts and content to various social media platforms including Twitter, Pinterest and Facebook.

http://buzzsprout.com:  If you are interested in creating podcasts, this is a good media site to host them.  You can get code to "rss" feed them to your website and they have a direct link to ITunes so once you are setup, all you have to do is upload them here and they appear automatically on ITunes as well within about 24 hours.

http://constantcontact.com:  One of the top e-mail marketing systems on the Internet with many tools, templates to support its users. It has a very strong auto-responder capability and does an excellent job of managing subscribers, opt-ins, opt outs, and subscriber activity tracking.

http://search.creativecommons.org : Find anything from photos and illustrations to videos that you can reuse for your own commercial online selling purposes. A great site to find things you need to complete projects yet protect yourself against copyright infringements.

http://ezinearticles.com/ : A good place to publish articles you create.  They do some marketing for you although not as much as they advertise, but it is a good holding spot for your articles and they have a number of tools/utilities you can use that help you to present your articles on your own site or blog.

http://www.facebook.com : The largest social media platform in the world. Originally built to connect with friends and family, they now offer sophisticated business pages and advertising capabilities. But to extend your reach so others can see your business pages, you have to pay for the advertising. Good news is you have several levels of "targeting" capabilities so you can prequalify who sees your page promotions.

http://faxzero.com: Send an online fax for free.

http://feedly.com : One of the better news services out there. It's well packaged, you can target the news you want to read and it has a good presence on other platforms such as Google Plus.

https://www.fiverr.com/ : Get cheap help for your business. You usually pay around $5.00 to $15.00 or so to get a myriad of services completed such as book covers for Kindle, introductions for YouTube videos, graphics work, etc. Check it out – it works!

https://www.flickr.com/creativecommons/ : A website where you can search for and download commercially usable photos and images. Flicker itself is a social media platform for your photos.

http://www.goodreads.com/ : A good place to view reviews on books and see people's comments on books. This is also a good location for authors to promote their books. Good search capabilities to find types of books you might be interested in reading.

https://plus.google.com/ : Google+ is a place to connect with friends and family, and explore all of your interests. Share photos, send messages, and stay in touch with the people, businesses and communities that you share interests with. Google has the largest search engine in the world; it owns YouTube so any YouTube videos you create automatically show up on your Google Plus pages and almost all other social media platforms out there integrate with it. Having a

Google Plus account as part of your business is a very good idea.

http://hootsuite.com: Hootsuite is a utility that helps you publish timed content to various social media platforms. It is a competitor to Buffer.com.

http://howtoguru.club : My training site. Contains training courses, articles I've written that can help you, links to YouTube videos I've created, my podcasts, and downloads that you could find useful to running your own business.

http://howtoguru.org: My recommended products site. This site contains books, software, electronics and other products that I have experience with and recommend as being good quality.

http://howto-guru.com: My blog and "lead capture" site. I use this to communicate interactively with my subscribers and to promote products I recommend. (Helps me keep the lights on here!)

http://iconfinder.com: A $9 a month subscription service to finding usable icons for commercial uses.

http://instagram.com: Instagram is a photo registering and sharing service. Snap a photo with your mobile phone, then choose a filter to transform the image into a memory to keep around forever. It has interfaces to Twitter, Flickrr, and Facebook.

http://istockphoto.com: A website that contains millions of royalty free images, illustrations, videos and music clips that can be purchased for commercial purposes.

http://LinkedIn.com: A major social media platform that also owns Slideshare.com. This site, originally used to post your business resume and background so you could find your next job, is now also a significant marketing platform.

http://livestream.com: A "Cloud" based broadcasting site that allows you to live stream events on any device. Also contains tools to embed the live streaming events on your website with the ability to replay them at any time.

http://logomakr.com: If you are trying to build a new logo for yourself, this is a good site to go to. Many images here you can get that could be incorporated into logos – most at no charge.

http://Lynda.com: Many, many Internet available training courses. If you want to learn a software tool, you can usually find a course or two on this site to help you.

http://mailchimp.com: An online e-mail generating and autoresponder service widely used on the Internet today. Many features and templates. Services start free but enhanced services, that you are bound to eventually want, will cost you. Competitor to Constant Contact and other similar services.

https://moz.com: 12+ tools—including Moz Analytics, Open Site Explorer, Followerwonk, and more—to track and improve your SEO, social, branding, link building, and content marketing efforts.

http://office.com: Site to purchase Microsoft Office applications.

http://oysterbooks.com: A $9.95 per month subscription gets you access to millions of downloadable books to read on your web browser, tablet or smart phone – they have a downloadable smart phone application. Also have books for sale on their site. If you want your book to appear there, you will need to work through "Smashwords" as they don't work with authors directly.

http://pdfescape.com: PDFescape is a free, online PDF reader, editor, form filler, & form designer. A new way to open and edit PDF files online, PDFescape frees users from the typical software requirements for using the de facto document file format. Completely online, PDFescape requires no more than a modern internet browser and an active internet connection.

http://www.picmonkey.com: PicMonkey makes creative tools for photo editing and graphic design.

http://www.pinterest.com: A top social media platform with millions of subscribers. Here, you can build "Boards" of content topics you are interested in, publish content to the site and to your boards by "Pinning" it, and provide link backs to your website and other content source locations. A very good platform for building connections with others and for pulling people to your business sites.

https://www.random.org: Tools and widgets installable on your website to help you pick random numbers.

http://reddit.com: Collects and collates into topic areas newsfeeds, articles and more for the use of its subscribers. A good site to be a part of and to promote your business.

http://semrush.com: Get insights into your competitors' strategies in display advertising, organic and paid search, and link building. Competitive keyword analytics tools.

http://seoranksmart.com: SEO Rank Smart specializes in providing Search Engine Optimization services. They work at getting your business ranked so customers can find you. They expand business brand presence and search engine visibility.

http://www.slideshare.net: Great slide presentations here – some you can republish - and a good social media site to belong to.

https://www.smashwords.com: Smashwords is an e-book distributor. They make it fast, free and easy for authors and publishers to distribute e-books to the world's largest e-book retailers. Authors and publishers retain full control over how their works are published, sampled, priced and sold. If an author wants to price a book at free, they have that freedom.

http://socialblade.com – A great site to check out statistics on other YouTube publishers. See their statistics, estimated earnings and more. Get yourself registered there as well!

http://Socialbro.com: The SocialBro platform enables advanced segmentation and audience insights into Twitter users – not just based on what they say or who they are, but how they think. The goal is to use this knowledge gained to generate campaign-specific, tailored audiences and serve relevant content to relevant people at the relevant time.

http://www.social-funnels.com: This site provides a Word Press plugin that can be used to help capture e-mail subscribers to your products. A useful tool if you are trying to build your e-mail lists.

http://Tumblr.com: The Tumblr platform is a place where people can blog with a view to getting many others to view their content. What you'll find on Tumblr are anything from stories to photos, television shows, links to people's websites, mp3 audios, and more. It has a good sized following so it is a place you should consider expanding your marketing presence to.

http://Twitter.com: Twitter is a social media platform that allows you to follow the "tweets" of others and to be followed in return. Once you build a follower base, you can create "tweets" that your followers will see and thus be able to promote your brand and be able to backlink them back to your site. For those wanting to share information with like-minded people, it is a good platform. But it has its limitations for those wanting to use it as a marketing platform. First, message lengths are very tight – you have to get your messages out in just a few words (although you can add an image to it to enhance it), secondly, Twitter has a 2,000 person cap that makes it difficult to increase your follower base beyond 2,000 people and third, advertising on Twitter is more expensive than say Facebook or YouTube.

http://unsplash.com: Get free, high resolution photo images here that are "creative commons" usable for commercial purposes on the Internet

http://www.wisestamp.com: The Wise Stamp site provides a platform with a variety of Email applications that on one hand lets users make a better use of their daily emails - adding a whole new level of functionality and interaction - and on the other hand enables publishers (social services and brands) to distribute their content and engage users in one of the biggest online markets – email.

http://YouTube.com: This is the number one video playback platform on the Internet today with millions upon millions of hours viewable. Owned by Google, it is tied in to their AdSense advertising platform and their search engine so you can earn revenue here and gain a lot of exposure. YouTube has a video promotion feature that can generate thousands of views of your content for only a few pennies a view so it is an extremely inexpensive advertising channel at the present. If you wish to create videos to promote your products, this is probably the best platform in the world to do this today.

**Dan Grijzenhout:** (Bio and resume at: http://howtoguru.org/about.htm )For close to thirty years, Dan has been a professional business and information systems consulting professional working to executive levels for both private and public sector organizations globally, a number of which were "Fortune" level enterprises. Dan has founded, operated and sold an online global payment services company that moves millions of dollars on behalf of its 100,000 plus account holders annually; he has been interviewed on the show "World Business Review" by former head of NATO and Secretary of State, General Alexander Haig, for his work in advanced digital and online telecommunications services and nation-wide online and card based "Loyalty" programs; and now works at writing to share his years of experience with others; helping those that wish to undertake entrepreneurial endeavors.

**Social Media Marketing, Content Creation and Authorship:** During the past year, 2015, Dan has focused nearly all his time and energy on building considerable hands-on expertise in social media marketing and social media strategy. To this end, he has built 3 websites geared to training people to be able to start, build and successfully operate online businesses. These websites include: A "Blog Site", a Training Course site and a "Mobile Technology – Responsive" Showcase site that allows him to showcase recommended "Affiliate products" along with his own content creation products which include three Amazon-Kindle published E-Books, over 40 published social media and business related training/learning articles, and over 70 published YouTube training videos, video podcasts and iTunes available podcasts on mobile platforms such as Smart Phones.

He has gained expertise in many online content creation toolsets including the full suite of Adobe Creative tools and Adobe Dreamweaver for website development; video and audio editing software; $3^{rd}$ party social media related website services and content creation partners; and most main-stream social communication platforms including Facebook and Facebook business pages, Pinterest, Twitter, Instagram, Google Plus, Reddit, Goodreads, Amazon Author Central, LinkedIn, Ezine Articles Publishing, Amazon-Kindle Book Publishing, Amazon Create Space and more. On these platforms, Dan has now amassed over 10,000 followers and subscribers and more are following him daily.

Dan's most recent work has been to build online training courses which he now primarily hosts on the Udemy.com training platform. See his profile and course list there at: https://www.udemy.com/u/dan-grijzenhout/ Dan currently has five courses on this platform, including two course that also cover the contents shared through this book.

## APPENDIX – FINDING DAN GRIJZENHOUT CONTENT ONLINE

Below are locations that you can find content created and posted by the author, Dan Grijzenhout.

http://howtoguru.org: My primary business site. This site contains my content, discounted Udemy course coupons, access to my books and: Software, electronics and other products that I have experience with and recommend as being good quality.

https://www.udemy.com/u/dan-grijzenhout/ Dan's profile page on the Udemy.com training site. Shows all of Dan's currently available training courses.

http://howtoguru.club : My training site. Contains training courses, articles I've written that can help you, links to YouTube videos I've created, my podcasts, and downloads that you could find useful to running your own business.

http://howto-guru.com: My blog and "lead capture" site. I use this to communicate interactively with my subscribers and to promote products I recommend. (Helps me keep the lights on here!)

https://www.pinterest.com/dgrijzenhout/: On Dan's "Boards" on this site, you can find content he has created such as his video podcasts, articles, some training videos and more. He has also pinned other 3rd party created content that he has found useful in building his online presence and in researching this book.

https://youtube.com/DanGrijzenhout123 : View Dan's created learning videos posted on YouTube.

https://plus.google.com/u/0/+DanGrijzenhout123: View Dan's content contributions on Google Plus https://www.facebook.com/Howtoguru.org : View Dan's "Howtoguru.club" business page on Facebook.

www.ingramcontent.com/pod-product-compliance
Lightning Source LLC
Chambersburg PA
CBHW060039210326
41520CB00009B/1195